# RATIONAL

# RUSTI

# REGULATION

*February 1981*

*Melbourne*

CIS Research Studies in Government Regulation **2**

# RATIONALISING RUSTIC REGULATION

## E. Sieper

THE CENTRE FOR INDEPENDENT STUDIES
1982

First published February 1982 by

The Centre for Independent Studies

National Library of Australia

Cataloguing in Publication Data

>Sieper, E. (Edward), 1942-.
>    Rationalising rustic regulation.
>
>    Bibliography.
>    Includes index.
>    ISBN 0 949769 02 9.
>
>    1. Agriculture and state - Australia. I. Centre for Independent Studies (Australia). II. Title. (Series: CIS research studies in government regulation; 2).

338.1'894

# Contents

# The Author

Edward Sieper graduated from the University of Sydney as a Bachelor of Economics in 1963. He has taught economics at universities in Australia, New Zealand and the U.S.A. and is currently employed by the Australian National University.

# Acknowledgements

Without thereby implicating them in any of its remaining errors or excesses, the author wishes to acknowledge the debt this revised version of the paper owes to the comments of George Fane, Fred Gruen, John Longworth, and Ross Parish, and to express his gratitude to Ross Parish for the not inconsiderable editorial effort expended by him in making the paper available, in its present form, to a rather wider audience than that for which it was originally, and rather too hastily, written.

# Preface

Undoubtedly the high point of the 1979 Annual Conference of the Australian Agricultural Economics Society was the appearance of Ted Sieper's paper, *Rationalising Rustic Regulation*. The paper's actual presentation was somewhat anticlimactic, since its distribution barely preceded its verbal presentation, and its length prevented both the audience from assimilating it and the author from conveying an adequate impression of its content. Indeed, it could be said that Mr Sieper displayed lamentable judgement of the requirements of a good, easily assimilable and discussible conference paper - for which error of prodigality we must remain deeply grateful to him. *Rationalising Rustic Regulation* is a highly original, insightful, and concentrated work, and a landmark in the discussion of agricultural policy in Australia.

The work's originality derives principally from the author's consistent attempt to understand agricultural interventions in a distributional perspective. That many regulations have the (presumably intended) effect of benefitting particular groups is, of course, not news. However, the distributional aspects of policies have remained peripheral to economists' concern, which has been largely with 'efficiency' aspects. Concentration on economic efficiency has had two unfortunate consequences as Sieper's work makes apparent. First, economists have tended to seek and to provide 'efficiency' explanations in cases where they strain credulity: this is rationalisation in the derogatory sense of the word. Sieper, in his introductory pages, exposes this sort of nonsense in a *tour-de-force* of selective quotation from the Rural Green Paper. Second, economists have dismissed as uninteresting or even irrational, or denounced, but seldom analysed closely, interventions that seemingly only promote economic inefficiency. It is most instructive to follow Sieper's numerous demonstrations that policies which seem misguided or irrational are, nevertheless, very understandable from a distributional perspective. For example, economists have consistently advocated on efficiency grounds that production and marketing quotas should be freely transferable, and on occasion have denounced as irrational the opposition to transferability. Sieper shows

vii

how various powerful interests stand to gain from quota non-transferability.

To view agricultural policy as the outcome of pork-barrel politics is not new, but it is not a viewpoint frequently taken by economists (at least in their professional capacity), and especially not by economists with Sieper's analytical powers. His paper demonstrates the capacity of 'technical' economic analysis to expose the presumed underlying political purposes of regulation. His methodology is essentially inductive and empirical: with respect to any regulatory instrument he asks the question, *cui bono?* and attempts to answer it by means of economic analysis. This approach differs from that of many practitioners in the burgeoning field of economics of regulation (or political economy, or public choice) who use economic concepts and modes of analysis to model political and bureaucratic behaviour. Clearly there is room for both approaches; furthermore they are interactive. For example Sieper throws out suggestions regarding the possible political purpose of various conventions and practices. Thus he notes that agricultural protection tends to take the form of giving each industry ownership of its demand curve, and suggests that this convention might serve to limit conflict over each industry's share of available transfers.

As well as illuminating the distributional effects of interventions, *Rationalising Rustic Regulation* provides numerous insights and pieces of analysis that are incidental to the main theme. The reduction of the complex of dairy industry interventions to a succession of simple tax-subsidy schemes is a case in point. It also contains a good deal of historical narrative and institutional detail, but this useful material is scattered through the text, which is organised on an analytical rather than an historical basis.

The original paper has been thoroughly revised for publication, and several errors corrected. Appendixes have been added to supplement terse pieces of analysis in the original text. An index has been supplied.

Mr Sieper is well known as an outstanding economist but a shy publisher. The Centre for Independent Studies is particularly pleased to be able to publish this work which has hitherto circulated only in *samizdat* form, but which nevertheless has acquired a considerable reputation.

**Ross Parish**

# 1

# Theories of Regulation

## The 'public-interest' theory

The traditional, and until recently formally unchallenged, theory of economic regulation interprets government intervention which differentially affects the fortunes of various industries and occupations as the product of altruistic efforts by the legislature to promote the public good.

While not blind to the existence of government policies designed to modify the distribution of income, this approach defines these as the proper function of a distributive branch of government operating through essentially neutral tax/transfer instruments specifically designed to be impartial in their impact across industries and occupations. With distributional questions disposed of in this way the ground is cleared for the 'scientific' rationalisation of the numerous observed instances of discriminatory government intervention in terms of economic efficiency. A multitude of sources of market failure are identified all of which imply the existence of potential gains from resource reallocation. Government intervention is then interpreted as the mechanism by which these gains are captured for society.

This efficiency theory of regulation has been vigorously argued in relation to government intervention in Australian agriculture, by the Rural Green Paper [17].[1] The Green Paper explains the observation that 'Australian governments are all interventionist, though to varying degrees,' by noting that 'their interventions, for the most part, seek to improve the manner in which the market operates or to compensate those adversely affected by its workings'. (3.7)[2] In

---

[1]   Numbers in square brackets refer to the references listed at the end of the book.

[2]   Numbers in parentheses identify paragraphs in the Rural Green Paper. Bold emphasis in the quotations below has been added.

1

particular, 'one objective of government intervention in the economy is to remove barriers to the **efficient working** of the market.' (10.9)

A variety of such barriers to efficiency is then identified along with the instances of government intervention designed to break them down. Thus there is the barrier to efficiency provided by the growing army of specialist middlemen:

> It is important that the signs the producer receives through prices accurately reflect the final market. Given the increasing involvement of intermediaries such as buying agents, traders, merchants, shippers, processors, manufacturers, wholesalers, and retailers, as well as governments, the chances are increasingly large that the message to the producer will be blurred. (6.5)

Government intervention in agricultural marketing, it is reasoned, is concerned to promote efficiency in the face of this complexity and to replace inertia by innovation.

> The growing size and complexity of the marketing sector makes it important to ensure continued improvement in **marketing efficiency;** the role of governments is to provide a framework for facilitating such improvements. (6.245)
> . . . . . . . . . . . . . . . . . . . . . . . . . . . . . . . . . .
> Where competition in the marketing system is not effective governments need to consider action to avoid **inertia, inefficiency** and **lack of innovation** by marketers and distributors. (6.252)

Similarly, since 'government policies are concerned with the **physical and technical efficiency** of the marketing process' (6.14), it follows that 'the existence of marketing boards will often help . . . the adoption of more **efficient** marketing systems.' (6.23)

Monopsony, described in terms of inequality of bargaining power, makes government intervention in agriculture an important part of its anti-monopoly policy. Since 'most farmers sell their products to firms much bigger than they are',(6.44) 'one objective of government involvement in price determination is again to provide bargaining support to producers where competition is inadequate . . . Examples include the sugar cane, milk and fruits industries.' (6.77)

Packaging and labelling laws are a further product of the

search for efficiency - 'on **economic efficiency** grounds the strict maintenance of standards of accuracy in the labelling of margarine is justified as is the application of strict hygiene standards on inputs to cooking margarine'. (3.97)    Legal restrictions on the form of contractual arrangements are justified by the fact that

> Governments obviously have an interest in ensuring that producers and consumers are not disadvantaged by vertical integration and that **resources are not used wastefully.**    There is a particular need for a minimum level of protective action for farmers involved in contractual relationships with processors. Various measures including legislation to specify the form of contracts . . . may be appropriate. (6.40)

Then there is the question of information, since, 'a further imperfection would result from lack of knowledge or information . . . The government may also wish to intervene when it considers it has better knowledge.' (3.14)    That the government **has** wished to promote efficiency in this way was later recognised:

> [The] kind of information . . . already provided extensively by various Australian and State marketing boards by State Departments of Agriculture as well as by the BAE [Bureau of Agricultural Economics] . . . is basic to the **efficient** functioning of the market. (6.132)

The market may fail also in respect of its dynamic functioning:

> The Government's involvement with assistance for farm adjustment is therefore designed to reduce the income problems which arise when help is not provided, and to lessen the **inefficiency** in the use of the nation's resources that the slow rate of adjustment implies. (10.17)

Moreover, because even when the market does not produce a rate of adjustment which is inefficiently slow it may well produce a rate which is inefficiently fast, there exists 'a justification on welfare and **efficiency** grounds for action to moderate the influence of market forces in order to ensure that unnecessary adjustment is not enforced.' (7.43)

Given this emphasis on the government as a powerful engine of economic efficiency, it is somewhat disappointing to find that another side of the efficiency rationalisation of government intervention identifies governments themselves as a source of market failure:

> Apart from the provision of public goods . . . a second set of reasons for intervention . . . concern the existence of imperfections in the system and include, in certain circumstances, the consequences of interventions by overseas governments in the agricultures in their countries.' (3.13)

More important still are the instances where our own government, by virtue of certain unfortunate interventions which have not been productive of efficiency, has fortuitously provided opportunities for efficiency gains to be harvested by further intervention. Thus because '[a] major source of imperfections results from the actions of government' (3.15), 'the case for government intervention in agriculture rests partly on compensatory action for intervention elsewhere in the economy.' (3.23) The major example is provided by the tariff whose effect is 'to attract resources away from the rural and other export industries . . . the result is a generally lower level of real (national) income.' (3.62) so that 'there is a case on economic grounds, a second best course of action, for providing some compensating protection i.e. assistance to the export sector.' (3.64)

Finally, the status quo in 'efficient' compensatory regulation is rationalised by the observation that '[i]n practice increases in protection using direct budgetary expenditures would have to compete with conflicting expenditure needs . . . This may put more emphasis on non-budgetary assistance measures, such as home consumption prices.' (3.75)

Clearly the efficiency theory of government intervention is capable of versatile application. Nonetheless it is limited by its failure to account for the process whereby the existence of market failure translates itself into the concern for economic efficiency that it presumes motivates government intervention. In this it suffers by comparison with the complementary theory of market efficiency which has, at least since Adam Smith, been emphatic that such efficiency as the market produces is the by-product of the selfish (wealth-maximising) concerns of private interests and not the outcome of any self-conscious concern for the public good.

## An alternative theory

An alternative theory of regulation - which we may for purposes of contrast dub the 'distributive theory' - is emerging which imputes this same wealth-maximising motivation to participants in the political process. Examples of this approach are to be found in the study by Pincus [29] of the United States tariff of 1824, in the work of Stigler [37] particularly his article 'The Theory of Economic Regulation' [36] and in later contributions by Posner [30] and Peltzman [28]. The distributive theory takes as its starting point the following observation:

> The state has one basic resource which in pure principle is not shared with even the mightiest of its citizens: the power to coerce. The state can seize money by the only method which is permitted by the laws of civilised society, by taxation. The state can ordain the physical movements of resources and the economic decisions of households without their consent. These powers provide the possibilities for the utilisation of the state by an industry to increase its profitability. ([36], p. 4)

This emphasis on the proposition that the observed behaviour of the state should be understood in terms of the incentives that its existence provides for the formation of interest groups that can effectively utilise its distributive powers, allies the distributive theory of intervention closely with an informal tradition, emphasising the 'pork-barrel' nature of politics, that has always shared an uneasy co-existence with the formal efficiency theory.

## Forms of intervention

It is the ambitious object of the new theory to account for the size and shape of effective political coalitions and for the direction and form taken by the transfers they are able to achieve; that is, for the observed characteristics of government intervention.

For the purposes of the present paper - which surveys some of the more important forms of government intervention in Australian agriculture - the chief interest of this new approach lies in the attention it focuses on the form taken by such intervention, viewing it as the product of a political balance struck between the interests of the industry receiving the transfer and those of the group being taxed to provide it.

If, for simplicity, we abstract from the possibility that government intervention is expressly designed to repair perceived market failures we confront the question, why do not benefited industries more frequently take their transfers in a lump-sum form? Since these by definition involve the least economic inefficiency, they would appear to have the appealing property that they maximise the gain to the industry from a given transfer.

One method of effecting lump-sum transfers, which recognises the political influence of an industry, is to link the transfers to some characteristic of the industry's members in the recent past. Though uncommon, this procedure is not unknown. Thus in 1936 the Commonwealth paid citrus growers a bounty of 6d per box on fruit exported in 1933.[3] In a similar vein, the revaluation compensation paid to apple and pear growers after December 1972 was based on a grower's average exports in 1971 and 1972, with a limit of $1,500 per grower. Again, payments to woolgrowers in 1970 were made to farmers who derived at least 30 per cent of their income from wool in 1968-69 and 1969-70, with a limit of $1,500 per grower.

Such transfers are incapable of being adapted to the changing characteristics of the group over time, without losing their non-distorting character. If, however, the attempt to achieve such adaptation is abandoned, so that the base of the transfer remains historically fixed, as is the case with various proposed market-entitlement or quota schemes discussed below, a non-distorting outcome is achievable.

An alternative form of lump-sum transfer is one based on the **current** status of the recipient as the member of the relevant group. Thus the recent Beef Husbandry Incentives Scheme with its limit of $2,000 per producer was, despite its title, broadly of this form. Clearly such transfers, if maintained over time, quickly lose their lump-sum character and to the extent that they are, for example, based on the payment of a given sum per producer may become severely distorting as they reduce the optimum scale of operation and as new entrants are attracted by the grant. Already such handouts have presumably distorted forms of farm ownership - it would seem prudent to nominally have one's operation

---

[3]     This form of payment was chosen to dispose of the three-fifths of the budget allocation in respect of the citrus export bounty which remained unused in 1936.

widely held. Finally, such grants, perhaps because they do not apportion benefits in proportion to influence within industry organisations, appear to find little favour with industry interests; wheat growers' organisations, for example, pressed strongly for the conversion of relief payments into a production bounty in the 1930s.

A further factor telling against lump-sum transfers is the concern the political process has to pay to the groups financing, and thus opposing, the transfer. Measures that are explicitly not lump-sum can be given the appearance of serving, if only indirectly, some wider set of interests commanding support - the promotion of 'development', of employment, or of the health of the balance of payments - and may thus invoke less opposition. In this way, schemes that involve interference with prices and thus, by generating deadweight losses, erode the gains to the industry for a given transfer, may nevertheless bring greater net gains to the group because they can be more cheaply sold to the opposition. In short, forms of transfer that involve greater economic inefficiency may up to a point provide a positive pay-off to an assisted industry.

Next there is the question of why we observe a strong preference for transfers to be linked to their own specific source of revenue. Thus the export subsidy on eggs is linked directly to the Commonwealth hen levy, the export subsidy on dairy products is financed in the main by a levy on domestic production, the assistance extended to the wheat industry in the 1930s was quickly financed in large part by a flour tax etc., while interventions such as tariffs, import quotas and regulatory home-price schemes clearly have this effect.

The result of such linking is to define a set of political property rights which provide the framework in which political competition for transfers, for the most part, proceeds. Roughly speaking, the rule that appears to have been observed in Australia is that each protected industry 'owns its own domestic demand curve' the elasticity of which bounds the size of the available transfer. Within that bound the size of the transfer actually attained will be governed by the need for the party in control of the political process to strike a balance between the marginal value to it of the transfer (in terms, say, of political support) and the marginal cost of the associated tax (in terms of the greater opposition or reduced support of those taxed).[4]

---

[4]    Peltzman [28] formally develops certain implications of this rule.

Given a rule that rigidly links the transfer and the tax, the direct opposition will be limited to the opposition of those taxed i.e. domestic consumers of the good. Thus the effect of such a linking convention is that it avoids a situation where powerful interests are placed in direct oppostion to one another - as would be the case where they competed for a common undifferentiated pool of Consolidated Revenue. Hence it may be that the economic purpose of the linking convention is to prevent the available transfers from being dissipated by competitive expenditures to offset powerful opposition.

Further, there is the question why many transfers are effected by means of administrative regulation - the home-price schemes discussed below being a prime example - rather than via an 'equivalent' set of explicit budgetary tax/transfer measures. Why, in Stigler's words, 'does an industry solicit the coercive powers of the State rather than its cash?' ([36] p. 4)

First, regulation provides a natural opportunity to link taxes and transfers automatically in the manner discussed above, while the Constitution provides (s.81) 'that all revenues or moneys raised or received by the Executive Government of the Commonwealth shall form one Conso-lidated Revenue Fund.' Second, regulation may provide the opportunity to engage in desired forms of discrimination (the example of a uniform price to all consumers in Australia is discussed below) that can be achieved through the budget only with difficulty. Third, regulation may provide an industry with cheaper opportunities to pay the rewards to industry leaders that are required to call forth an appropriate supply of organisational effort. And fourth, where transfers are explicitly made in cash they must, broadly speaking, be raised in that form also. Thus, though regulation will often involve an additional regulatory cost, that cost may be worth bearing where the implicit taxes implied by regulation, because of their lower 'visibility', invoke less opposition. If considerations of visibility are important we should expect that an industry capable of extracting a cash transfer from the budget would wish to see that transfer paid in a manner that generates further 'hidden', i.e. non-budgetary, assistance. (Several apparent examples of this phenomenon are discussed below.) Similarly, we should expect to see especially strong pressure to keep the value of the transfer hidden when it is of a lump-sum form and therefore has no 'public interest' justification. Since lump sum transfers arise from quota schemes this will have implications for quota transferability.

Finally, it should be emphasised that distributive considerations can be expected to condition the form that intervention takes, even where such intervention is designed explicitly to correct obvious market failure. Buchanan and Tullock [3] illustrate how the political choice between direct controls and pollution taxes will be influenced by the distributional implications of the alternatives. Not surprisingly, they conclude that industries will prefer direct controls not only to the tax alternative, but also, where such industries are not already regulated, to the status quo. The use of acreage restriction in Australian rice growing, ostensibly to handle salinity externalities associated with the large quantities of irrigation water applied, provides an example.

# 2
# Import Protection

Given the ubiquity of import protection it is not entirely surprising to find that where Australian agricultural industries have been subject to import competition they have been able to secure the protection of tariffs, embargoes, quarantine restrictions, and 'understandings', concluded between governments, that export to Australia will not be attempted (e.g. those with New Zealand affecting trade in dairy products and lamb). Moreover, such protection has been extended not only to 'natural' import-competing agricultural industries (i.e. those which in the absence of intervention would share the market with a significant volume of imports) but also to industries located in the export or non-traded goods sectors of the economy, whenever the object has been to give such industries a home price above import parity.

The first Commonwealth tariff extended generous import protection both to sugar (₤6 per ton or about 50 per cent *ad valorem*) as part of a combination of measures designed to secure the repatriation of the kanakas and their replacement by white labour, and to dried vine fruits (3d per lb or about 100 per cent *ad valorem*) the production of which had earlier been encouraged by Victoria in order to persuade farmers to take up land in her heavily subsidised irrigation schemes.

By the time of the Brigden Inquiry in 1927 the list of minor agricultural products protected against import competition was long and included hops (30 per cent), maize (17 per cent), nuts (25-100 per cent), bananas, tobacco, onions, and potatoes.[5] The fact that many of the products on this list were produced chiefly or exclusively in a single non-industrial State (bananas, maize, tobacco and nuts in Queensland, hops in Tasmania) is suggestive of a degree of log-rolling on the tariff between those States advancing industrial, and those seeking agricultural, protection.

High Australian transport costs made it difficult for

---

5    See [12] , Appendix N.

regionally-concentrated items of production to compete against imports in distant parts of the Australian market. Moreover, the policy of protection for Australian shipping, consummated with the exclusion in 1921 of vessels not observing Australian wages and conditions from the coastal trade, further eroded the natural shelter of such commodities and provided grounds for compensating tariff protection.[6]

That the pure strategy of devoting resources to opposing the claims for protection advanced by all and sundry is dominated for most interest groups by a mixed strategy which gives most weight to the promotion of the group's own narrow interest, quickly impressed itself upon the Country Party when it entered the Federal coalition government in 1922. Its leader, Page, quickly coined the phrase 'protection all round' and set about persuading the revenue-tariffist wing of the Party, led by Gregory (representing Swan) to accept the need to join the 'vicious circle'.[7]

Where that meant a home-consumption price for export industries,[8] - as it did for the sugar industry when it moved to an export basis in 1922 and as it did for the dairy industry from 1926 - the import protection necessary to sustain local prices above import parity was quickly forthcoming in the form of a sugar embargo (still in place) and, when in 1927 imports from New Zealand threatened the Paterson dairy plan, a rise in the tariff on butter from 2d to 6d per lb (still the current rate).[9] Where home-price arrangements have since been introduced (e.g. eggs, wheat), the necessary exclusion of imports has been achieved under the quarantine regulations (except of course for high protein wheat imports in 1957-58 and imports of eggs for scientific purposes).

## Non-tariff barriers to imports

Quarantine and health regulations, in many respects an 'ideal' form of protection, frequently combining high purpose with total import prohibition, have also been used to exclude potatoes, on which an import embargo imposed in 1928

---

[6]   See [34] pp. 400-411.
[7]   See [15] p. 231.
[8]   As early as 1907 the dried fruits industry had commenced to export on a home price basis, from behind its high tariff wall.
[9]   Imports are effectively excluded despite the low tariff. The agreement with N.Z. mentioned above assists in this.

remains in force (except in times of extreme shortage) and to establish long quarantine periods for imported cheese.[10] Less subtle non-tariff barriers to import competitition include the requirement that imported margarine be coloured pink and the ban on filled-milk imports imposed in 1961.

The States also make effective use of quarantine, health, and packaging and labelling laws to shelter their local producers against interstate competition. Examples relevant to agriculture are the interstate restrictions on fruit marketing,[11] the restrictive effects of labelling laws affecting margarine[12], and the protection Western Australia provides its citrus growers by banning the sale of the Vitamin C supplement 'Tang'.

Notable instances of State protectionism held by the High Court to infringe upon s.92 include a Victorian embargo on Tasmanian potatoes (1935), South Australia's prohibition of the sale of margarine manufactured from ingredients not first submitted to its official inspection (1966) and New South Wales' attempt to oust a Victorian dairy company selling milk in that State (1975).[13]

## Product inter-relationships

Close inter-relationships among commodities on either the side of demand or of supply will on occasion give certain industries a keen interest in the tariff protection achieved by others. Thus producers can be expected to oppose increased protection accorded their important intermediate inputs. By contrast, the producers of those inputs will have little or no interest, where their protection is simply provided by means

---

10   The 1939 Royal Commission into the Fruit Industry in N.S.W. felt secure in condemning the potato embargo (which had led to a retaliatory embargo by New Zealand on fruit and vegetable imports from Australia) as scientifically unjustified. At the same time it had no difficulty in recommending that the use in fruit cakes of synthetic cherries made from swede turnips be prohibited by the N.S.W. Department of Public Health. See [32] pp. 117-18, pp. 423-25 and p. 215.

11   See [20] pp. 87-88.

12   See [39] pp. 64-65.

13   The cases referred to are respectively *Tasmania v. Victoria* (1935), *O'Sullivan v Miracle Foods* (1966) and *North Eastern Dairy v. Dairy Industry Authority of N.S.W.* (1975).

of the tariff, in supporting increased protection to such final outputs. Of course both groups can make common cause in pressing for an increase in effective protection to both activities simultaneously. It is a political function of local-content schemes to institutionalise this commonality of interest.

In contrast to the situation where protection is provided by the tariff alone, a local-content scheme gives both parties an interest in pressing for increased protection to final output since under such a scheme this automatically increases protection to the input suppliers as well. Accordingly, the incentive for components manufacturers to devote resources to the quest for higher input tariffs and for the producers of final output to expend resources in opposing them, if not thereby removed, is at least rather diminished.

Local-content arrangements have applied to both tobacco and cotton. Concessional entry of imported tobacco leaf has been available to cigarette manufacturers who use at least a statutory percentage of local leaf in **every** product that they manufacture. The statutory percentage has increased steadily from 2.5 per cent in 1936 to 50 per cent in 1966. However the three local manufacturers currently maintain local content at 57 per cent on a 'voluntary' basis even though it appears that they could do better by importing all their leaf at the full rate of duty. The situation here, as elsewhere, appears to be one in which it is not so much the letter of the legislation as the threat it embodies that conditions observed behaviour. (The local-content arrangements for cotton are discussed below pp. 15-18.)

On the side of demand, where an import-competing good exhibits substitutability in consumption with another product whose price is not determined by world markets, protection accorded producers of the former also serves the interests of those of the latter. Thus the 65 per cent tariff levied on imports of orange juice in June 1977 cannot have been incongenial to fluid milk interests in the dairy industry. Imports of orange juice fell from 21 million litres in 1976-77 to 6.3 million litres in the first eleven months of 1977-78. The rapid increase in the retail price of this commodity has been tempered only, and at some cost to flavour, by the oversight that exempted mandarine (tangerine) juice from the tariff increase. Imports of the latter for blending purposes have grown from 300,000 litres in 1976-77 to over 2 million litres in 1977-78 - an episode that has left a nasty taste in many mouths.

# 3

# Production Subsidies

The rule that protection is produced for a political market in which **existing** industry interests provide the demand and governments the supply, is subject to qualification. Political entrepreneurship in the promotion of **new** industries and **new** methods or areas of production, as exemplified by Deakin's sponsorship of Victorian irrigation schemes in the 1880s and more recently by the Ord River Scheme, is not unknown.

The *Bounties Act* 1907 and the *Manufacturers' Encouragement Acts* 1908-1912 offered bounties (usually at a rate of 10 per cent *ad valorem)* for the production of flax, jute, rice, rubber, coffee, tobacco leaf, and cotton as well as to a number of non-existent manufacturing activities, e.g. galvanised iron. Such bounties to 'infants' (and 'embryos') allowed a proper concern for 'development' to be displayed by the young Commonwealth Parliament at negligible cost, or risk of cost, to Consolidated Revenue. They also offered scope for indirect industrial regulation since, as with tariffs enacted at that time, such bounty assistance was made conditional upon the certification, by Parliament or an appropriate industrial tribunal, of the 'fairness and reasonableness' of the wages paid and conditions of employment provided by the recipients.[14]

The scope of bounty assistance was further extended in 1922 when the Country Party under Page, newly entered into coalition with the Bruce government, was successful in securing the deletion from the Massy Greene tariff of 1920

---

[14] With tariffs the procedure involved the imposition of a matching excise (production tax) with provision being made for its remission where fair and reasonable wages were paid. The famous 'Harvester judgement', was brought down under these provisions of the *Tariff Act* 1906 and was influential in converting Labour parliamentarians, many of whom had voted to limit the height of the original Commonwealth tariff, to the virtues of protection (see [34] pp. 397-98).

of a number of agricultural inputs (wire netting, fencing wire, galvanised iron, tractors, and sulphuric acid) whose production was then encouraged by means of bounty.

As the range of commodities subject to bounty widens and as significant rates of bounty-protected production are achieved the political inexpediency of direct assistance becomes more acute. The search for disguised forms of assistance, which render the bounties implicit and provide them each with their own source of implicit tax revenue, leads directly to the tariff where import-competing production is involved, to local-content plans where intermediate inputs are to be protected and to home-price schemes for export industries with a sufficient home market. There remain, in the traded goods sector, only the 'pure' export industries - those with negligible or non-existent home markets. For these, we may safely predict, the avoidance of bounty assistance will pose a thorny problem.

The political concern to avoid direct bounty payments where this is possible and to constrain them sharply where it is not, is well illustrated by the case of an industry, cotton growing, which received such Commonwealth assistance continuously from 1922 to 1971.

**The cotton-growing industry**

An Australian cotton-growing industry emerged briefly during the American Civil War. Sporadic attempts by the Queensland Government to revive it thereafter were joined by a 10 per cent Federal bounty under the *Bounties Act* 1907. In 1920 the Queensland Government introduced a guaranteed price. The Tariff Board, which was to develop a particular enthusiasm for the industry, conducted an inquiry in 1922 which led the Commonwealth to share equally with the States the bounty cost of the price guarantee. All production at this time was exported.

When efforts by the Queensland Government to push the whole of the bounty funding onto the Commonwealth were succesful in 1926,

> The Bruce-Page government arrived at the conclusion that the policy hitherto adopted of assisting the cotton-growing industry on a purely export basis was fundamentally unsound in view of the higher production costs in Australia as compared with other countries . . . (and) . . . propounded a policy of developing the Australian cotton industry primarily on a home

15

consumption basis by deciding to create within Australia a market for locally produced cotton.'[15]

Thus the problem created by the inevitable and growing budget costs of assisting a purely export-oriented 'high-cost' industry was to be solved by creating a couple more high-cost import-competing industries further down the Leontief chain.

In pursuit of this objective the 1926 *Cotton Bounty Act*, while continuing the bounty on seed (i.e. unginned) cotton, made provision for the first import duties on cotton yarn. As a further incentive to the establishment of a local spinning industry a bounty was provided on local yarn containing at least 50 per cent Australian cotton - this proviso being included because local cotton was of higher quality than would otherwise have been required by yarns suitable for domestic manufactured cotton goods. Finally, tariffs were introduced for the first time on a range of finished cotton goods.

In 1929 the Tariff Board again reported in glowing terms on the prospects for cotton. However, rather than raise both the seed cotton and cotton yarn bounties, as recommended by the Board, the Scullin government continued the Bruce-Page approach, making provision for their phased elimination by 1936. Simultaneously it imposed the first import duties on raw cotton, increased the import duties on locally-produced yarns to an almost prohibitive 55 per cent (35 per cent preferential) and undertook to provide whatever increased protection to yarns and to manufactured cotton goods might prove necessary. Local spinning expanded so rapidly that by the latter half of 1933 imports of protected cotton yarns were only 2.5 per cent of local consumption.

By 1933 the Tariff Board had lost its ardour for expanded cotton growing. Under the influence both of the bounty on seed cotton and the tariff-protected home price (which was extracted from local spinners by the operations of the Queensland Cotton Marketing Board) raw cotton production had increased to levels not again to be attained until the early 1960s. In consequence exports remained at over half local production despite the growth of domestic spinning. Bounty costs remained high and might increase. A new policy was therefore propounded under which the now influential local cotton-using industries were to be expanded and raw cotton exports were to be curtailed. First, the price of local cotton to spinners was to be reduced to import

---

[15]    T.H. White, Minister for Trade and Customs, House of Representatives, 13 July 1934, quoted in [11] p. 515.

parity. Any raw cotton which could not be obtained from the Queensland Board at this price could be imported duty-free. Second, and in partial imitation of the arrangments obtaining for Queensland sugar, the seed-cotton bounty (now converted to a raw cotton basis) was to be paid only on estimated domestic requirements plus a contingency reserve of 20 per cent, was to move inversely to the Liverpool spot price and was not to exceed 6½d per lb.[16]    Tariffs on yarn and on manufactured cotton goods were raised yet again.

The extent to which, under this regime, raw-cotton production languished while the output of the domestic cotton-using industries grew, is indicated by the fact that throughout the 1950s cotton production averaged less than a quarter of the annual rate attained in the early thirties and amounted to less than 5 per cent of the cotton consumption of local spinners in those years.[17]

The establishment of the Australian cotton-growing industry in its present form occurred in the 'sixties with the development of wet-land cotton farming in the Namoi region of N.S.W.   It owed little to government intervention, taking place at constant world prices and in the face of a sharply declining rate of bounty payment.[18]    By 1968 the industry had returned to an export, and by 1972-73 to a net export, basis.  In 1971 the bounty was removed.[19]

The conflict between the political desire to provide (gross) industry assistance and the political distaste on all (relevant) sides for readily visible forms of protection has normally been resolved in Australia by recourse to comparatively obscure home-price arrangments.   The attempt to create for cotton the home market that is a precondition for such obscurantism was a spectacular success which nonetheless failed entirely, over thirty-five years, to thereby establish the significant cotton-growing industry that was its original object.   Its legacy is a segment of manufacturing industry whose own demands for protection quickly attained a

---

[16]    During the war years the seed cotton guarantee was reintroduced without limitation on eligible production.

[17]    See [5]

[18]    The aggregate bounty payment was limited to $4m in 1963.

[19]    Spinners now 'voluntarily' agree to purchase their requirements locally at import parity while competition among exporting ginners is prevented from driving prices down to export parity by an informal quota scheme which shares the local market among them.

momentum, and have latterly displayed a singular durability, of their own. Whereas the original 1926 Bruce-Page tariffs designed to establish the local production of towelling and knitted cotton goods both stood at 35 per cent (20 per cent preferential) these are now estimated by the Industries Assistance Commission (IAC) to be 50 per cent and 85-100 per cent respectively (quota protection equivalent), while the cotton-using sector as a whole now operates with rates of effective protection ranging from 40 per cent (cotton yarn) to 300 per cent (bed linen).

## Maximising the gain from bounties

It seems safe to assume that where an industry is able to extract a certain sum from Consolidated Revenue by way of a bounty it will be concerned more to maximise the advantage it extracts from the bounty than to minimise any associated social costs. Where the output subject to bounty has different uses in consumption or enters as an intermediate input into alternative production processes a set of **differential** subsidies to its consumption in these alternative uses can be a powerful means to this end.

Consider an industry whose output is, for simplicity, taken to be in perfectly inelastic supply. A simple production subsidy would then accrue entirely to producers and would involve no deadweight losses. Now suppose that the product is an intermediate input entering (in fixed proportions to output) into alternative processing activities of which we shall, again for simplicity, assume there are only two.

A uniform subsidy to the processing industries on their use of the input will then leave the mix of processed production unchanged and will again accrue in lump-sum fashion to the producers of the input. If, instead, the use of the input were subsidised at differential rates as between the activities this will expand production of the favoured activity and increase its producer surplus while causing production, and producer surplus, in the other sector to contract.

It is clear that, provided the elasticity of demand for the input differs across the processing sectors, there will be some pattern of differential subsidies that is preferred to a uniform bounty by producers of the input. Indeed, the optimum differential between the subsidies (given that a sufficient sum of bounty is available) is that which produces the mix of processing activity which would be established by a discriminating monopolist selling the input.

Thus we have the rule that the industry should seek to have the subsidy applied exclusively to the use of the input in that activity whose derived demand is the more elastic, up to the point where the marginal revenue from sales to each sector is the same. Thereafter, if still greater amounts of bounty are available, it would wish to see further subsidies applied at the same rate to the product in both its uses.[20]

An example of how an industry may in this way be able to turn a production subsidy to its greater advantage, albeit at some greater social cost, is provided by the history of the dairy subsidy introduced during World War II.

Following the recommendation of the Tariff Board, advised by C.R. Sheehy, General Manager of Commonwealth Dairy Produce Equalisation Committee Limited (CDPEC) the company administering dairy equalisation, the dairy bounty introduced in 1942 flowed only to milk entering butter and cheese production. With the prices of condensary products (condensed, evaporated and powdered full cream milk) fixed under wartime price controls, the supply of dried milk promptly dried up.

The Dairy Produce Control Committee formed under the National Security Act was now faced with the problem

> of meeting the demands of condensed and dried milks for the Fighting Services . . . So alarming were the shortages of condensed milk that it was found necessary to divert fresh milk from certain centres in Victoria . . . This necessary diversion involved city milk and cheese factory supplies in many cases, with attendant disturbance of normal trading practice and the retarding of cheese manufacture which was also vitally important. The curtailing of city milk supplies called for a re-apportionment of the depleted quantity among milk vendors. Realising that such action called for the attention of an authority possessing a knowledge of retail trade, steps were taken . . . to have regulations passed which clothed the Victorian Milk Board with the necessary powers to divert milk etc. . . . This particular phase of control, namely supplies of milk for condensaries, now comes within the ambit of the Controller of Dairy Products, who reviewed the whole question of supply and demand and accordingly planned a long-range policy.[21]

---

[20] The theoretical basis of this conclusion is set out more formally in Appendix 1.

[21] Dairy Produce Control Committee, *Annual Report*, 1943 (quoted in [40] p. 56.)

Hasty adjustments were made to the controlled prices of condensary products and in April 1943 the coverage of the subsidy was extended to include them.

In 1952 the dairy industry was again successful in having the subsidy restricted to milk entering the production of butter and cheese.[22] The effect has been to expand the production and export of these products at the expense of the production and export of condensary products, with the result that the return on a given quantity of milk exported in manufactured form has not been maximised.[23] Provided, however, that the derived demand for milk entering condensary production was the more inelastic - a likely supposition since the value added here is greater - milk producers stood to gain from such, bounty enforced, price discrimination.

Moreover there are circumstances where fine elasticity comparisons are redundant. Suppose that in the model outlined above the producers of the input (milk) form a coalition with one processing sector (butter and cheese). We may then take the change in the sum of the returns to producers of the input and the producer surplus generated in that one processing sector as the approximate criterion of gain to the coalition. In these circumstances it will pay the 'industry', now defined to include one processing sector, to seek the exclusive subsidisation of the input in its own processing activity, regardless of the relative elasticities of derived demand for the input across uses. And it will pay to demand the continuation of such exclusive subsidisation as the total bounty available rises, up to the point where the marginal social cost of the production mix-distortion equals the marginal transfer of surplus from the sector excluded from the subsidy (i.e. up to the point where the price, net of bounty, paid by processors equals the marginal revenue from sales of the input to the unsubsidised sector).

In connection with the dairy subsidy it is not irrelevant to observe, therefore, that while butter is overwhelmingly and cheese signficantly produced by farmer-owned co-operative dairy factories, proprietory companies, many of them overseas owned, dominate the condensary sector. This aspect of the logic of the exclusion of condensary products from the bounty appears to have escaped the authors of the

---

[22] Between 1962-63 and 1974-75 a small export subsidy was again paid on processed milk products (including condensary products).

[23] The assumption is made here that elasticities of export demand are equal across manufactured milk products.

'Submission by a Group of Agricultural Economists' to the 1960 Committee of Enquiry into the Dairy Industry, who argued that 'The **unintended** effect of the present system is therefore virtually to tax exports of whole milk in any form other than butter and cheese.' (emphasis added) [24]

---

[24]   [9] p. 127.

# 4
# Export Subsidies

In that they raise consumer and producer prices by a like amount, export subsidies duplicate for export industries the effects of tariff protection for industries that compete with imports. Yet, when set alongside the tariff, export subsidies appear as a comparative rarity.[25]

Part of the explanation would seem to lie, first, in the fact that the tariff augments, while the export subsidy depletes, Consolidated Revenues and, second, in the ease with which a tariff can be represented as being chiefly a device to promote the interests of nationals at the expense of foreigners while an export subsidy is unpromisingly suggestive of foreign aid. Against this, the particular advantage of an export subsidy to an export industry lies in the 'hidden' assistance it provides through the matching rise in the home price that follows in its wake. This gearing factor will be larger the lower is the proportion of production exported, the more highly integrated is the domestic market and the higher is the elasticity of substitution in local demand between the choicest grades that often dominate exports and the bulk of production.

An export bounty was provided by the *Bounties Act* 1907 on dried (non-vine) fruit. Exports of beef were subsidised in 1922 and 1923, of dried vine fruits in 1924, canned fruits between 1920 and 1929 and fortified wines between 1920 and 1928. In each case the subsidies were to small exporting industries and, with the exception of that on dried fruit, were

---

[25] Export industries would presumably find life sweet in a 'Metzler' world where the elasticity of export demand is so low (specifically, less than the domestic marginal propensity to consume exportables) that export **taxes** provide them with protection while by contrast import **subsidies** are needed to protect import-competing industries. (See L.A. Metzler, 'Tariffs, the Terms of Trade, and the Distribution of National Income', *Journal of Political Economy*, February, 1949)

in the nature of short-term emergency assistance.

A subsidy to citrus exports was paid in the 1930s initially as a price guarantee and subsequently as a fixed bounty. Interestingly, certain growers' organisations in both N.S.W. and Victoria opposed the bounties, arguing that they would bring government control and claiming that a subsidy on the small proportion of high quality fruit exported would have little impact on the prices realised for the bulk of production consumed domestically.

Since 1971 subsidies in the form of price guarantees have been paid on apple and pear exports. The effect of the subsidies on domestic apple prices has been minimised by the fact that export production is concentrated in Tasmania and Western Australia, while internal trade is restricted by freight rates from these States comparable with those to Europe and by the barriers to imports erected by the eastern mainland States.

The abolition in 1976 of the Meat Export Charge imposed in 1973 to recover the costs of export meat inspection, represents an export subsidy to this industry which the budget estimates place at $32.4m for 1978-79.

**The dairy bounty**

A major exception to the rule that large budgetary subventions are difficult for an industry to achieve and harder yet to hold has been the dairy bounty. Introduced in 1942 as a temporary wartime measure to sustain production in the face of controlled domestic prices and export prices set lower still, this temporary expedient endured until phased out by the Labor Government between 1973 and 1975, and has since re-emerged in 1977-78 in the guise of underwriting assistance, estimated by the budget statements to equal $17m in 1978-79. Originally $2m per annum, the bounty rose to $35.6m per annum at its peak in 1951-52[26] largely because, with the Commonwealth at that time guaranteeing dairy farmers a price equal to export realisations, the States, administering price control after 1948, were free to indulge consumers at the Commonwealth's expense. In 1956-57 the bounty was fixed at $27m per annum, at which level it remained until 1965-66 when it was augmented by devaluation compensation payments.

Though not always recognised as such, the dairy bounty, when combined with the equalisation machinery of the

---

[26] In nominal terms the highest rate of bounty (including devaluation compensation) was $47.6m in 1969-70.

private company CDPEC Limited, to which it was paid, produced over the decade 1956-1965 an outcome not significantly different from a simple export subsidy. Indeed, given the tangled web of dairy regulation, with its changing formulae for calculating the rate of bounty and its aggregate amount, with its guaranteed prices based on 'costs of production', with its successive Stabilisation Plans and above all with its administratively involved system of equalisation, it is remarkable in retrospect that the post-war years neatly subdivide themselves into four distinct periods, in each of which an elementary non-regulatory analogue of the whole complex of controls exists; based in the first three periods on the bounty payments alone.[27]

Period I: 1947-1952. During this period post-war price controls held the price of butter below export realisations by some 28 per cent on average. Producer prices however were only 1 per cent above export prices on average and the largest divergence was 5 per cent. Clearly the net effect was broadly equivalent to a **consumption subsidy** with the qualification that, since butter was rationed locally, the removal of regulation and the payment of an explicit consumption subsidy of equal budgetary cost would not have kept measured consumer prices quite so far below export returns.

Period II: 1953-1955. In 1953 the domestic price was allowed to rise to approximate export parity (which itself fell). Consumer prices were only 3 per cent above export prices on average over the period, the largest divergence being 4.5 per cent. By contrast producer prices were 27 per cent above export prices on average. The net effect was therefore very close to that of a **production subsidy.** Since an export industry should always prefer an export subsidy to a production subsidy of the same value the dairy industry arguably made 'inefficient' use of the bounty. The likely explanation is that, given the sharp rise in consumer prices in 1953 with the termination of the implicit consumption subsidy, political constraints limited the ability of the industry to immediately convert the bounty into a **de facto** export subsidy.

Period III: 1956-65. This is the period during which the system was equivalent to an **export subsidy.** When the long-term contract with the U.K. expired in June 1955 the fall in

---

[27] The data on which the calculations below are based are contained in CDPEC Limited, *Forty-Third Annual Report of Directors*, 1977.

export realisations was accompanied by a rise in consumer prices to approximate equality with producers' returns. Consumer prices were only 0.7 per cent above producer prices on average over the period with the largest divergence being 5 per cent.

Although the industry possessed the administrative machinery to implement a home-price scheme, that is to raise consumer prices above producer prices, no legal impediment to interstate sales existed. Commonwealth bounty payments were available only to producers operating inside equalisation and the industry acted as if constrained by the opportunities for profitable interstate trading outside equalisation that a home price set significantly above the equalised return would have provided. While the payment of the bounty sustained the complex 'voluntary' equalisation machinery the same outcome could have been achieved by an export subsidy of equal budgetary cost.

Period IV: 1966-1973. Only from 1966 to 1973, when the dairy bounty was phased out, did the combined system of regulation plus bounty (and devaluation compensation) exhibit the characteristics of a **home-price scheme**. Moreover the extent to which local prices were raised above those which would have been permitted had the bounty and devaluation compensation been paid as an explicit export subsidy was relatively modest. Consumer prices were only 9 per cent above producer prices on average, the largest divergence being 14 per cent.

The whole episode illustrates the flexibility of administrative regulation. One is left to wonder whether the gradual transformation of a consumption subsidy into a production subsidy and thence into a subsidy on exports could have been so readily achieved had it been necessary to perform it in the open. Certainly the Commonwealth Committee of Enquiry into the Dairy Industry would then have been unable to argue, as it did in 1960 when discussing the relationship of the dairy scheme to the General Agreement on Tariffs and Trade

The operation of the dairy industry stabilisation scheme does allow export prices to exceed or to fall below domestic prices . . . However the bounty is paid on domestic consumption (plus a safety margin of 20 per cent to counter the vicissitudes of climate and season) and this tends to moderate exports rather than stimulate them. ([9] p. 66.)

## Price discrimination among export markets

The principle that when a bounty is available to an industry it should wish to see it used to establish profitable patterns of price discrimination that would otherwise be difficult to enforce, was discussed above in relation to production subsidies. Similarly, export subsidies provide obvious scope for price discrimination to be practised among export markets.

Thus the citrus bounty of the 1930s was originally paid to compensate growers for the loss of the New Zealand market in 1932 when that country retaliated against our potato embargo. When exports to New Zealand resumed in 1936 the bounty lingered on and was paid in 1936 and 1937 on exports to all markets. Since the New Zealand market was dominated by Australian exports while other markets were not, this was an error which was corrected when, between 1938 and 1940, the subsidy was paid only on exports to markets other than New Zealand.

A more recent example is provided by the Apple and Pear Stabilisation Scheme institututed in 1971 and the joint Commonwealth/State Supplementary Assistance Scheme for Apples added in 1974. Under these schemes export subsidies are provided only on shipments exported 'at (Australian exporter's) risk'. Since the Apple and Pear Corporation ([APC], formerly Board) prohibits 'at risk' shipments to markets other than Europe (including the U.K.) for apples and to markets other than Europe (including the U.K.) and North America for pears, the effect is to restrict supplies to, and maintain prices in, the newer and nearer South-East Asian export markets where Australian supplies form a much larger proportion of market supplies.

Compared to a system of overt discrimination by destination this device imposes a clear regulatory cost. It induces the substitution of 'at risk' for forward selling in one set of markets and prevents any 'at risk' sales that might occur in the other.[28] Thus forward sales to the U.K. which in the 'sixties accounted for 40-50 per cent of all sales have dropped to negligible proportions.

---

[28] While there may in principle be scope within any given market for practising profitable price discrimination among export sales according to contract type *per se*, it is clear that a system which involves the elimination in that market of one or other mode of selling must involve a net loss.

The IAC report on the industry [20] which argued

APC export regulations have distorted and restricted the choice of method of sale available to exporters. In the Commission's view the industry's interests would be better served if exporters were able to use their commercial judgement unfettered. (p. 69)

recognised this regulatory cost. In arguing further that

It might be expected that, because of the different shares of the risk and finance costs carried by the importer and exporter . . . the returns to exporters from at risk sales would on average be greater than those from foward sales . . . this has not been the case over recent years. (p. 74)

the report apparently failed, however, to recognise that this discrepancy arises precisely **because** the scheme permits covert price discrimination to be practised between traditional markets, where 'at risk' sales have been dominant in recent years, and other markets, the returns from which produce the observed higher forward-sales returns.

However, the attraction of subterfuge is not the only explanation of why this regulatory cost is borne by the industry. In common with other arrangements of its type the scheme providing for the bounty payments has been invested with the trappings of price stabilisation. The bounty takes the form of supplements to bring export returns up to predetermined guaranteed prices established by variety and provision is made for grower contributions should the price guarantee fall below the export return. In this context the significance of the restriction of the scheme to 'at risk' shipments is that growers are thereby allowed the opportunity to switch back to forward selling should it happen that the guaranteed prices have been set too low, so that grower contributions threaten.

For pears, where growers at large have had occasion to avail themselves of this splendid option, the proportion of sales 'at risk', that is inside the scheme, has averaged 82 per cent of all sales to the relevant markets (Britain, Europe and North America) in the years when the bounty was payable while the proportion of forward sales, outside the scheme, to these markets has averaged 85 per cent in those years when grower contributions were required.[29]

---

[29]    See [20] pp. 95 and 144.

# 5
# Export Controls

The comparative narrowness of the channels carrying international trade has historically made such trade an attractive target for taxation and administrative regulation. Nonetheless, the present highly comprehensive degree of government control over Australia's agricultural export trade developed slowly.

The regulation of Australia's export trade had its beginnings in tentative Colonial efforts to administer the growing volume of butter, cheese, and frozen meat exports that developed in the 1890s. In 1895 Queensland compelled the inspection and certification of meat for export. In the same year Victoria, which had since 1887 made export inspection a condition of eligibility for export bounties on factory-made butter, succeeded, against strong opposition, in making official export inspection mandatory. Similar Queensland legislation proposed in 1897 failed to overcome similar opposition and was not introduced until 1904. New South Wales, in typically restrained fashion, limited its initiatives to the establishment of a Board of Exports, again in 1895, which offered grading and certification services to interested exporters, while the South Australian government created a State agency through which producers could, if they chose, export to London.[30]

The new Commonwealth hastened slowly to assert its Constitutional powers over the export trade, the *Commerce Act 1905* requiring only that produce for export must be marked with a truthful trade description and permitting, for a limited range of commodities, the regulatory enforcement of specific trade descriptions. However by 1927 it could boast:

A very effective system of supervision over primary products and other goods exported has been built up during the last twenty years. Under the *Customs Act 1901-25* and the *Commerce (Trade Descriptions)*

---

[30] See Reeves [31] Chapter VI pp. 371-86.

*Act* 1905-26, the Commonwealth exercises supervision over the preparation, manufacture, grade
quality, packing and labelling of practically all
foodstuffs (except wheat and flour) exported, also
boots, shoes and leather.   From time to time regulations are made under the Acts setting out the
requirements that are to be observed.   The products
to which these regulations apply are butter, cheese,
eggs, milk and cream (dried, powdered and pre-
served), meat and meat products, poultry, rabbits and
hares, fruits (dried, fresh and canned), pickles, honey,
maize, plants, seeds, vegetables, sauces, jams and
leather. [31]

## Quality control

How is the extreme concern with compulsory standards of
quality in the agricultural export trade to be accounted for?

First, high quality is something always difficult to be
against, and high standards are often advocated as an end in
themselves - the Rural Green Paper [17] going so far as to
advocate that, 'it would be desirable to have a uniform set of
minimum standards of quality . . . to give domestic consumers
the same quality as overseas consumers'. (6.213)

Second, there is the externality argument articulated by
the Rural Green Paper that, 'failure to meet accepted
standards by one exporter or one shipment could adversely
affect a number of exporters or indeed all of the export
trade' (6.209)   Though often advanced, by interests seeking
regulation in other areas (e.g. occupational licensing), this
argument presupposes an unusual degree of naivete on the
part of foreign buyers.   However, it gains greater weight,
when applied to agricultural exports, from the consideration
that health and quarantine regulations provide foreign
governments with a ready means of extending disguised
protection against all Australian exports of a commodity
should some shipments prove deficient.

Third, in some instances Australian government
certification of quality and enforcement of standards in
processing may be insisted upon by overseas governments as a
condition of entry into export markets.

Finally, government-provided export inspection and
certification services, to the extent that they substitute for

---

[31]   Statement by T. Paterson, Minister of Markets, 22
December 1927, (quoted in [11] p. 465).

private expenditures to this end and are not charged for, constitute an export subsidy which is of greater value to industries with a substantial and unregulated home market than the budgetary subventions on this account ($38m for 1978-79 for the Commonwealth) would, themselves, suggest.

**Export boards and their funding**

The establishment of the battery of Commonwealth Boards and Corporations which now control the agricultural export trade began in 1924 with the creation of the Australian Dairy Produce Board. Based on earlier New Zealand legislation establishing Meat and Dairy Export Boards, the relevant Bill (which provided that the enabling Act would not come into operation unless a majority of growers voted in favour) appears to have been a somewhat reluctant response by the Bruce-Page government to industry demands for the establishment of a Board with far wider powers including the power to fix domestic prices in line with the 'costs of production'.

In similar fashion and in rapid succession Boards regulating the exports of Dried Fruits (1925), Canned Fruits (1926) and Wine (1929) were established on the vote, respectively of growers, canneries, and wineries. By contrast, proposed Export Control Boards for Meat (1925) and Apples and Pears (1924, 1927) failed to command majority producer support and were subsequently introduced [Meat (1935), Apples and Pears (1938)] without polls of producers being taken.

Statutory boards exercise their powers under executive regulations recommended by the board but introduced by the responsible Minister. Thus the establishment in January 1925 of the Dairy Produce Board required the creation of a Department of Markets (forerunner of the present Department of Primary Industry) which assumed responsibility for the administration of the growing area of regulatory export control.

With the introduction of Australian boards for wheat (1939), eggs (1947), and honey (1962) and with the export of sugar and coarse grains controlled at the State level, only wool and the newly-emergent cotton export trade remain as important exemptions from direct export regulation.

Significantly, the Australian Wool Corporation (AWC) proposed in 1973 that it should become the sole wool exporter, rationing the commodity to users at stable prices whenever these threatened to rise. In 1977 the AWC commenced to purchase wool direct from growers, partly to establish its competence as a monopoly trader and also to counter the growth of the private-treaty trading system that has occurred since the introduction of the reserve price scheme in 1970. In the case of cotton the BAE in 1963 urged that, 'if the Australian cotton industry develops it would be desirable for a central authority to establish and maintain quality standards.' ([4] p. xi)

The range of powers possessed by these export boards and corporations is wide. At one extreme lies the Australian Honey Board which has control only over honey voluntarily placed at its disposal while at the other stand the Australian Wheat Board and CSR which possess monopoly rights to the export trade, the latter as agent of the Queensland Sugar Board. Most other boards exercise regulatory control over the timing of shipments, quality, prices etc. and possess the power to license exporters, while many have acquired the power to trade on their own account (e.g. the Australian Meat Board [now Australian Meat and Livestock Corporation], the Australian Dairy Corporation, and the Australian Apple and Pear Corporation.)

Such boards may be of value to an industry in negotiating lower rates of freight or insurance or in securing reduced rates of duty on Australian exports to certain markets. All these were successes claimed by the Dried Fruits and Dairy Boards shortly after their establishment. Moreover, an export board may on occasion be useful in promoting industry demands for wider regulation. By way of example consider the role of the Australian Dairy Produce Board in relation to margarine quotas. The Board,

> decided at its annual meeting last July [1938] to ask the Commonwealth Government to have legislation passed to prohibit the manufacture, import, and sale of margarine manufactured from imported vegetable fats; and to provide that any margarine manufactured from locally-produced vegetable fats shall be coloured in a manner that will make it entirely different in appearance from butter.
> On several occasions the Board . . . [has] . . . urged the State and Commonwealth Governments to bring in the necessary legislation to protect the dairying industry against unfair competition from margarine, and at the last annual general meeting of the Board regret was expressed that, although some States had been active in endeavouring to suppress this unfair competition, no action of a uniform

character had been taken by the States. The Board
sincerely hopes that the dairying industry will receive
the protection such an important industry deserves.
(*Annual Report*, 1938. Quoted in [40] p. 38.)

Another example is provided by the efforts on behalf of the
industry of the Australian Canned Fruits Board. The Board
has recently obtained Government approval for a statutory
two-pool plan which it has developed to replace the secure
voluntary home-price scheme organised by the industry with
the assistance of the Rural Credits Department of the
Reserve Bank. The new scheme will give the Board trading
powers and will establish it as the regulatory authority for
both home and foreign markets.[32]
However, the distinct possibility exists that such boards
will be motivated to exercise their export licensing powers to
restrict entry to the export trade, thus reducing competition
and innovation among exporters and inhibiting the development of non-traditional export markets. Where the domestic
price is unregulated, and therefore linked to export realisations, the consequences will be felt by producers on local as
well as export sales. Certainly the issue of the relative
representation of exporters and producers on such boards
remains a lively one (e.g. the debate over the composition of
the Australian Meat Board [AMB] in recent years).
All export control boards levy charges to finance their
operations and to provide funds for research and promotion.
Where a home price scheme is not in operation or where such
a scheme rests on a shaky voluntary basis, the base of these
levies has important implications for producers' returns. We
should expect an industry to prefer these charges to be levied
on domestic consumption. Failing that, a levy on production
would clearly be preferred to one on exports. It is not
surprising therefore to find that, while most export boards
originally raised funds by levying charges on exports, there is
a clear trend towards the replacement of these charges by
taxes on domestic consumption or production.
The Wine Board has since 1929 received the proceeds of a
levy on grapes used in the production of wine, the Canned
Fruits Board which has been funded by an export levy since
1926 has since 1963 also received the proceeds of an excise
on domestic consumption, the Honey Board raises the bulk of
its funds from a tax on domestic honey sales but also levies a
small charge on exports. In 1964 the source of funds for the

---

[32]    See *Australian Financial Review*, 1 February 1979, p. 9.

Meat Board was switched from exports to a slaughter levy and while the old Apple and Pear Board was funded by an export levy the new Apple and Pear Corporation is funded by a levy on all fruit sold on both local and export markets.

These changes have important implications for the incentives under which such boards operate. To take an extreme example imagine a board whose activities are confined to export promotion and are funded by a tax on domestic consumption. If the local price net of tax is directly determined by the export return, the industry has an incentive to seek the expansion of the board's export promotion activities up to the point where their gross marginal productivity is zero (if this is possible within the limits of the revenue-maximising consumption tax). Certainly we should expect to see the changed basis of the boards' funding produce an expansion in the scale of their activities.

## Controlling the volume of exports

With respect to the aggregate quantity, as distinct from the quality, of the export of a commodity, board regulation offers the opportunity compulsorily to expand or to contract export volumes.

Undoubtedly the former motivation, that the Commonwealth's export powers could be used to increase exports and thus draw supplies away from the home market, was much in the minds of the advocates of the early Commonwealth Boards. Indeed, in the case of dairying (1934-36) and dried vine fruits (1928-36), home-price schemes were established under the sanction of State legislation which limited the quantities which could be sold intrastate and of Commonwealth legislation which insisted that an export quota be filled before interstate sales were permitted.

However the success, in 1936, of the recusant dried vine fruit grower James in having the Privy Council declare that s.92 of the Constitution bound not only the States, but also the Commonwealth, to respect the 'absolute' freedom of interstate trade, commerce, and intercourse, ended the era of *de jure* export expansion under the Commonwealth's international trade power [s.51 (1)].

The alternative possibility, the use of export regulation to contract aggregate exports of a commodity, is subject to the not inconsiderable economic, rather than legal, impediment that the elasticity of demand for our exports is customarily substantially larger than that for home market supplies.

An early proposal for export restriction which foundered on this rock was that advanced by the Australian Dairy Produce Control Board in November 1932. Under the voluntary Paterson home-price scheme, instituted by the dairy industry in 1926, the volume of Australian butter exports to the U.K. increased by about 200 per cent over the years 1926 to 1932. Believing, no doubt correctly, that the fall in the London price from 161s per cwt in 1926-27 to 86s 6d per cwt in 1932-33 was not entirely unrelated to this export expansion, the Board proposed exercising its powers to restrict annual exports by 20 per cent. The extreme hostility of the local industry to this proposal suggested that it was in no doubt as to the relation between marginal revenues in the two markets, and led the Board to develop a new proposal whereby it would restrict Australian exports by 6 per cent on condition, first, that the United Kingdom government would restrict other foreign supplies to the market by twice this amount, and second, that the Australian government would buy up the butter diverted by the Australian quota. Neither party accepted the offer.

Since then, Australian export restriction has typically been confined to situations where such control has been accepted under obligation to the rules of international commodity cartels to which we may belong at the time (wheat and sugar provide occasional examples) or to situations where home prices, fixed on the basis of some 'cost of production' formula or other, have temporarily remained below sharply rising world prices, so that control of exports has been necessary for domestic rationing to be avoided (again wheat and sugar during the commodity boom of the early 1970s afford examples).

## Discrimination among export markets[33]

There remains the possibility of using export regulation to discriminate among foreign markets.

Suppose that demand elasticities for Australian exports differ among markets because, for example, our exports form a large proportion of market supplies in some regions and a small proportion in others. Assume also that transport costs or other barriers allow some scope for driving Australian f.o.b. prices to these markets apart. In these circumstances a tax on exports to markets where demand is relatively

---

[33] The economic analysis underlying this section is set out in greater detail in Appendix 2.

inelastic combined with a subsidy, paid out of the proceeds, on exports to markets where demand is relatively elastic can provide a self-financing scheme capable of extracting for domestic producers gains from price discrimination among foreign markets. With the domestic price unregulated, the rise in average export realisations will produce a corresponding rise in home prices. Alternatively, a board with monopoly trading powers could achieve this outcome by operating on quantities directly. Either way, export control provides the industry with a 'hidden' export subsidy extracted from foreigners.

It is of some interest to ask how such a scheme, run to maximise the producing industry's interests, compares with a scheme of exploitation of foreigners organised to maximise the 'national' interest.

Suppose in the first instance that the export controls are operated to maximise the average export price realised on any given quantity of exports (i.e. to equate marginal revenues across export markets). Equality is maintained between domestic consumer and producer prices, as is required by a scheme operating in the 'national' interest but these are driven **up** where the nationally optimum scheme (involving the taxation of exports to all markets in which foreign demand is responsive) would drive them **down** - the paradoxical 'Metzler' case excepted - to equality with the (equalised) marginal revenues from foreign markets. In short the industry scheme **expands** while the optimum scheme would **contract,** or (in the limiting case where some category of export demand is infinitely elastic) leave unchanged, the aggregate volume of exports of the commodity.

Given this perverse implication for aggregate exports, there remains the question of whether a board maximising the industry's interests will in fact be motivated to distribute exports across foreign markets so as to equate marginal revenues among them.

The answer here is that it will, provided that at the point where foreign marginal revenues are equated the implied marginal revenue on the domestic market lies below this; or, equivalently, that demand on the home market remains more inelastic than the demand for our exports on the most elastic foreign market (both elasticities evaluated using the common consumer and producer prices). It seems safe to suggest that this condition will normally be met in practice and that in consequence export control boards will not be inhibited in their relative exploitation of foreigners by the fear of thereby drawing a larger volume of supplies from the domestic market than would be in the interests of the industry.

What examples of such discrimination exist in practice? The monopoly exporters, the Australian Wheat Board and CSR, no doubt believe that they are effective in this respect[34] although in both instances the home-price implications discussed above are masked by the independent regulation of that price.

In the case of the regulatory boards (where the conduct of the export trade remains in private hands) there is in addition to the Apple and Pear Stabilisation Scheme discussed above (pp. 26-27) the example of the Beef Diversification Scheme operated by the Australian Meat Board since 1968. Here rights to a U.S. market quota for Australian beef (the quota effectively being imposed by the U.S. but granted in expiation to Australian nationals) are shared among Australian meat exporters by the Board in proportion to their exports to other markets. The effect of the scheme is broadly equivalent to the tax/subsidy combinations discussed

---

[34] Thus in evidence to the IAC Sugar Inquiry, CSR argued

> . . . we have had a steadily expanding export market and in that market we would assert that we are price makers rather than just people who accept price insofar as it may be just quietly got on the market - which means of course that we see ourselves as pretty aggressive marketers.

- a contention from which the following convenient implication was quickly drawn:

> I should say that other manufacturers of raws around the world would very much like to know what the costs were of such an aggressive competitor as this industry is in the international market. We contend strongly that they should be denied this marketing advantage. Nevertheless we make the point that costs have been given to the Committee and will be given to independent people of high repute such as yourself and your colleagues. (Minutes of Evidence pp. 918-20, IAC report: *The Sugar Industry,* March 1979.)

The question of whether the Australian Wheat Board would realise more from (say) a grand annual wheat auction than from overseas sales often negotiated below ruling world prices, remains open.

above or to a system in which the Board would auction the U.S. quota rights and pay an export subsidy out of the proceeds.

However, since the U.S. quota is fixed and it does not pay us to restrict exports to the U.S. further, and since the quota is granted to Australia, the Beef Diversification Scheme differs from a scheme of price discrimination among export markets in that it neither alters the distribution of a **given quantity** of exports across markets nor alters the realisations on a **given quantity** of exports in those markets. Its motivation is simply to capture the windfall gains which would otherwise accrue to Australian holders of U.S. quotas and distribute them to beef producers in a form (an implicit export subsidy) which raises domestic consumer prices.

A variation closer to the spirit of price discrimination among export markets would arise where a foreign country, as part of its import quota system, imposes an Australian quota but gives the import rights to its **own** nationals. In this case the tax/subsidy scheme discussed above (or its equivalent) could be administered to capture part of the quota profits for Australia. Although demand in the quota market is perfectly inelastic up to some price, so that no switching of given exports among markets is involved, this example does involve price discrimination in the sense that the Australian realisation on the quota market is raised above that on other export markets by such a scheme. It has been suggested that there may be some scope for the AMB to play this game with respect to the Japanese and Canadian markets. (see [14])

In 1976 the Board proposed the subsidisation of beef sales to non-traditional export markets with the subsidy financed by a levy on all beef exports. Had this proposal been adopted by the industry, a fully-fledged system of price discrimination among export markets could have in principle been brought into effect.

While the present regulatory allocation of U.S. beef quotas by the AMB generates regulatory costs (as discussed in [14]) the industry has been careful to resist suggestions that it adopt an auction system. In part this may be accounted for by the possibility that if visible auction revenues were generated pressures would emerge for them to be devoted to ends other than the subsidisation of exports. Certainly one should not expect the industry to view with favour the possibility canvassed by Freebairn and Gruen ([14] p. 34) that 'the money could be returned to producers through a subsidy of slaughter or processing costs or of research and promotion

37

grants', since such a production subsidy on beef would cancel the rise in domestic consumer prices which is an attraction of the present system. Moreover, still less favourable destinations for any auction revenues might readily be found - including for example their use to offset the large beef export inspection costs presently borne by the Commonwealth.

# 6
# Pooling

We will define equalisation as the process by which returns to producers are averaged across markets when price discrimination is enforced among them, and pooling as the process by which returns from the sale of a commodity during some time period are averaged across participating producers. Though the two are frequently associated in practice it is clear that neither implies the other. Thus equalisation without pooling occurs when price discrimination is enforced through tax/bounty measures or when, for example, export quotas are allocated which producers must either fill (e.g. the dried fruits and dairy schemes of the 1930s) or can earn (e.g. the Beef Diversification scheme of the 1970s).

It is a characteristic of equalisation without pooling that returns will vary among producers and among marketers with the result that they operate under the same incentive structure, as regards excellence and specialisation in production and marketing, as would exist in its absence.

Pooling without equalisation is equally possible. Clearly some measure of pooling arises informally under many marketing arrangements due to economic limits to the frequency with which prices are changed. Formal pooling arrangements, usually involving an advance to sellers on delivery and one or more adjustments as sales realisations accrue throughout the season, have also existed on a voluntary basis at various times and for various commodities. The wheat pools run in the individual States during the 1920s and 1930s provide an example as do the competing pools run by some exporters of apples and pears and the voluntary oats pool currently operating in Western Australia.

Since intra-seasonal price fluctuations can be large and since in non-auction markets a spread of prices can be observed at any point in time, participation in a pool represents the implicit purchase of an insurance contract whose premiums and payouts combine to guarantee the average pool realisation. Insurance has its costs of production, among them the moral hazard it generates (e.g. costs of pool administration will typically make the recognition of fewer grade differences profitable) and the adverse selection it induces (e.g. 'low risk' sellers, skilled at timing their sales to secure high prices, will tend not to participate).

The history of the voluntary wheat pools attests to the presence of these costs (pool realisations were in general below average realisations outside the pools), and the steady decline in the patronage they received over the years 1921-22 to 1938-39, leading to their virtual extinction in all states except Western Australia (compulsory pooling was retained after World War I in Queensland), is suggestive of the conclusion that competing forms of insurance against undesired fluctuations in consumption, (for example the use of the capital market) were available to producers at lower cost. (See [13] p. 232)

Interestingly, the declining proportion of the wheat crop handled by the voluntary pools was accompanied in N.S.W. and Victoria by increasing agitation for the introduction of compulsory pooling under the aegis of State Marketing Boards. In part this may be explained by the fact that the growers' organisations ran the declining voluntary pools. A further explanation is that the State legislation, which provided for the establishment of marketing boards on a vote of the growers, compelled such boards to pool producers' returns. Thus the prospect that board control might bring government guaranteed prices or gains from price discrimination was inextricably interwoven with the pooling issue. Nonetheless, proposals for board control of wheat failed to command the requisite majority on each occasion they were put to the vote. (In N.S.W. a poll of wheat producers was taken each year between 1928 and 1931.)

## Attenuation of price differentials

Compulsory pooling of producers' returns on an Australia-wide basis has tended to involve the elimination or attenuation of market price differentials for quality in the prices paid to **producers** and the suppression of market differentials in the prices to **consumers** both across Australia and across seasons. Such practices may be presumed to involve social costs and have often attracted criticism on such grounds. However, since the gains from eliminating such costs should be capturable by the producers who are producing output of 'inappropriate' quality, are undertaking 'excessive' transport and storage of the product etc., the problem of accounting for the existence of such practices remains.

The system of dairy equalisation administered by CDPEC since 1935 involved a series of separate product pools. In the important case of butter, returns were equalised in a single pool without regard to product quality. The significance of the world price differentials thus suppressed is indicated by the prices paid by the New Zealand Dairy Products Marketing Commission which in 1960 offered a premium for 'choicest' butter of 8 per cent over second, and 26 per cent over third grade. (See [9], p. 43)

The 'quality problem' thus manufactured in Australia was handled by State legislation which prescribed minimum price differentials between grades which dairy factories were required to observe when purchasing milk or cream. This regulatory solution produced its own difficulties, among them being the tendency for the legislated minimum differentials to remain constant in nominal terms in the face of rising milk prices, and the problem of enforcement as dairy factories were encouraged to compete for supplies by illegally 'grading up' inferior milk.

A series of conferences of dairy interests was convened between 1953 and 1955 to wrestle with the problem. The upshot was that CDPEC resisted the introduction of end-product price differentials, no agreement could be reached on the desirability of widening the eroded legislative cream price differentials, attempts to talk quality up (quality improvement campaigns by the States) failed and more Draconian recommendations, such as the suggestion by the 1954 Conference of Commonwealth and State Dairy Officers, that all States should legislate for heavy monetary penalties on factories which failed to convert at least 85 per cent of choicest cream into choicest butter, were not acted upon.

The persistence of 'inadequate' penalties for low quality butter was noted by the 1975 Board of Inquiry into the Dairy Industry in Victoria [1] which records that while second grade butter converted to butteroil for icecream manufacture yielded the pool $25 per cwt less than the equalisation value, the producer of such butter was paid only $1 per cwt below the equalised price.

Although the existence of such low penalties for low quality output has continued to be regarded as a defect of dairy equalisation, drawing criticism from both the 1960 McCarthy Committee and the 1975 McFarlane Board of Inquiry, (see [9] p. 44 and [1] Second Report p. 23, respectively) the temptation to assert the collective irrationality of the dairy industry should be resisted, at least until its status as a discriminating monopolist is taken into account.

Thus, suppose there are two grades of butter, with the second grade being used for manufacturing purposes, and assume that supplies are allocated so that the marginal revenue of each grade is equal to its **given** export price. If the **supply** of each grade is equally elastic (in the sense that a simultaneous one per cent increase in the producer price of both grades would generate an equi-proportionate rise in the supply of each grade) then an equalisation authority motivated to maximise aggregate producer surplus should establish a relative producer price for the two grades equal to their relative marginal revenues. Under these circumstances relative world prices therefore provide an indication of the appropriate producer price relativity. By contrast, the large difference cited by the McFarlane Inquiry, between the domestic price of manufacturing butter and the equalisation value, is a reflection of the dramatic difference in **demand** elasticities between, and thus in the prices charged in, the two domestic markets. As such, it is irrelevant to an assessment of the appropriate relative producer price between grades.

Moreover, if it is the case that the supply of manufacturing butter is relatively inelastic (in the sense that a simultaneous one per cent rise in the producer price of both grades would raise the relative supply of first-grade butter) then it will be rational for the equalisation authority to set a relative producer price for manufacturing butter which is higher than its relative marginal revenue (relative export price). This arises because the additional revenue extracted from the domestic markets via price discrimination will be more effective in raising aggregate producer surplus if it is biased towards the grade that is in relatively inelastic supply.

Where a minority of growers produce high grades of a commodity and the production of these is relatively inelastic with respect to the price differential, as appears to be the case with prime hard wheats, it can be in the interests of the majority to oppose the recognition of such premium output by the pool. Certainly the Australian Wheat Board (AWB) has moved slowly to establish additional grades, which would attract quality premiums for growers, for wheat marketed within Australian Standard White, and such 'political' pressures may also operate to retard the establishment of otherwise profitable varietal segregations.

At the other end of the the spectrum, the production of

certain high-yielding stock-feed wheats has been prohibited by the States, on the recommendation of the AWB, since they cannot be accommodated within the provisions of the existing legislation and would pose a threat to the home-price arrangements if developed outside it. Similarly the AWB has set dockages for off-grade wheat well below the price differentials ruling in the market, in part to inhibit the growth of private trading outside the Board. (See [8] pp. 28, 74, and 111.)

**Producer gains from pooling**

As noted above, Australia-wide pooling arrangements have tended to combine uniform prices to consumers with the pooling of returns among growers.[35]

The encouragement given to excessive transport of the commodity within Australia (or across time where consumer prices are prevented from varying according to season) represents a social cost which, other things equal, falls upon the pool. There appear to be several reasons why producers might choose to bear this cost.

---

[35] It is worth observing that there can be difficulties in duplicating by budgetary means the uniformity in consumer (and producer) prices across Australia that can be achieved by pooling. Thus s.51(ii) of the Constitution provides that the Commonwealth may make laws 'with respect to taxation, but not so as to discriminate between States or parts of States' while s.51(iii) provides for laws with respect to 'bounties on the production and export of goods, but so that such bounties shall be uniform throughout the Commonwealth'.

Although numerous examples exist of budgetary measures which appear to violate these injunctions (e.g. the former petrol subsidy to country areas, the income tax zone allowance, etc.) and although s.96 which provides that 'the Parliament may grant financial assistance to any State on such terms and conditions as the Parliament thinks fit' allows the spirit of s.51 to be readily circumvented (e.g. Tasmania was effectively exempted from the flour tax of the 1930s by rebating it under a s.96 grant), it remains the case that this is an area where laws of taxation or bounty could only achieve with difficulty what regulation can apparently accomplish with ease.

The first arises because the movement to a uniform consumer price across Australia will produce a transfer from consumers in exporting States to consumers in States that import from the rest of Australia. This transfer necessarily runs in the **opposite direction** to the transfer across States implied by the pooling of producers' returns (here producers in exporting States gain at the expense of producers in importing States). Thus, to combine pooling with a uniform consumer price may help to buy political support for the scheme as a whole in States where producers lose relatively from pooling. In a similar vein, a uniform price to consumers when a home-price scheme is established for a product the production of which is heavily concentrated in a single State (e.g. Queensland sugar) serves to limit the rise in the price to consumers most in those States distant from the centre of production (Western Australia and Tasmania in the case of sugar) where prices were previously highest.

A further consideration is that there may be gains from price discrimination among States that producers can capture by moving towards a uniform Australian consumer price. Whether such gains exist is of course an empirical question. However if we assume first, that **individual** demand curves for the product do not differ systematically across Australia and, second, that the State-wide demand curves are linear across the range of movement to a uniform Australian price, the question of presumption can readily be examined.

Under these circumstances there are gains to the industry as a whole from attenuating the consumer price differences due to transport costs while to eliminate them entirely involves neither gain nor loss.

To see this suppose there are two States. In a free market, consumer prices will be higher in the importing than in the exporting State by the transport cost differential, $T$. If there were an equal number of consumers in each State a uniform price, $p$, would imply uniform consumption, $x$, and the price change in moving to a uniform price would be equally distributed across the States. Clearly the rise in gross industry revenue from a uniform price,

$$(2px - \{[p + \tfrac{1}{2}T][x - \Delta x] + [p - \tfrac{1}{2}T][x + \Delta x]\}),$$

will be exactly offset by the transport costs, $T\Delta x$, on the additional quantity, $\Delta x$, exported.

If consumers are unequally distributed across States the price change will be unequally distributed also, being smaller the larger the State. However in its effects on gross industry revenue this will be exactly countered by the fact that the smaller price change in the larger State falls on a larger volume of consumption, so that the conclusion that the change in gross revenue just balances the additional transport costs still holds.[36]   If there is a zero net gain in moving to a uniform price it follows that a partial movement in this direction will bring a net gain.

The dairy pools have been based on the principle of a uniform wholesale price within Australia, constant throughout the year, so that processors selling on the local market have been liable in the first instance for the difference between the wholesale price and the equalisation value.   Any costs of transport and storage were rebated to processors or wholesalers and were charged against the pool.   Since the actual costs of performing these operations could not be ascertained with great accuracy and since the payment of actual costs provides no incentive for cost minimisation, hundreds of individual transport and storage allowances were set as maxima by CDPEC.

In this way the **administration** of a uniform price to consumers operated to create deadweight losses **additional** to those necessarily implied by such price discrimination *per se*.   These additional deadweight losses arose because

---

[36]   In general the change in gross industry revenue is equal to the integral of the difference between marginal revenues in the two States across the change in consumption in moving to a uniform price.   With demand linear the marginal revenue in a State is $a_i - 2b_i x_i$, where $a_i$ is the price intercept and $b_i$ is the slope of the State demand function.   As a function of price, marginal revenue is therefore $2p_i - a_i$ and, being independent of $b_i$, is thus independent of the number of consumers in the State.   The change in gross industry revenue is therefore $\frac{1}{2}\{(a_2 - a_1) + 2T\} \Delta x$ where 1 is the importing, and 2 the exporting State.   With no differences in individual demand curves across States $a_2 = a_1$ and the gross gain in industry revenue $T \Delta x$ just covers the additional costs of transport.   Clearly a price differential of $\frac{1}{2}T$ between the States will under these circumstances maximise net revenue to the industry.

Moreover, any differences among States which work to make individual demands more inelastic at a common price in exporting than in importing States $(a_2 > a_1)$ will produce positive net gains from the establishment of a uniform price, and conversely.

processors were placed in the position of free riders, given an incentive to 'play the system' of allowances by undertaking unnecessary transport and storage operations where these were privately profitable.

In the second of its recent reports on the industry the IAC showed an awareness of these problems but argued that

> the system of allowances, which has been developed under equalisation allows processors to extract most of the costs of storage and distribution from the pool . . . Thus, equalisation has operated in a manner which could allow processors to obtain a larger share of any assistance provided to the dairy industry through the domestic price differential than would otherwise have been available to it (sic). ([19] p. 39)

The IAC attempted to explain the fact that the uniform Australian price regime administered by CDPEC had then endured for forty years, by the observation that 'the equalisation pools are presently controlled by processors'.

This argument, that a system which encourages free riding favours processors as a group, appears to confuse the relative gains to those processors skilled at exploiting the rules of the game, or in a position to bend those rules to their benefit, with the position of the group as a whole. To the extent that the administration of a uniform consumer price has generated deadweight losses these have fallen on the pool, and thus, for a given price to consumers, on both farmers **and** processors. Indeed it may be the case that no processor has derived a **net gain** from the administrative deficiencies of the system. Moreover, given that the system has effectively taxed some processors in favour of others, there appears no reason to believe that such transfers, by themselves, would particularly disadvantage dairy farmers.

In the case of wheat, storage costs are pooled across producers Australia-wide and are not reflected in prices to consumers by time of sale. Transport costs by contrast are allowed for in prices to both producers and consumers within States but according to simple rules of thumb (e.g. growers are docked for transport from sidings to terminals). As between States the significant features are that transport to Tasmania is subsidised by the pool while consumer prices in Western Australia are also effectively subsidised by the system because export parity is higher in that State - a consideration which is reflected in a special allowance to Western Australian producers but not in the price charged

Western Australian consumers.

Since bulk storage costs are charged against the pool any incentive to combine private with bulk system storage is removed (except when, as in 1978-79, an exceptionally large crop induces the Wheat Board to pay private storage allowances).

Moreover, because the bulk handling authorities are administered separately by the States but charge their costs against the common pool an incentive towards the free-riding behaviour which characterises the dairy arrangements is introduced. The failure to charge consumers prices differentiated by season produces the same implications for user storage and the timing of production decisions that pooling produces for growers. Predictably, the proportion of wheat handled by private traders outside the Board diminishes as the season progresses.

Similarly, since transport costs are not charged to growers and users in the manner which would be established by the market, the location decisions of both parties are presumably somewhat distorted. Undoubtedly the formerly grey interstate trade, now black (see footnote 50, p. 58), and the black intrastate trade carried on outside the Board have operated to reduce some of these costs while creating others, e.g. unnecessary haulage.

The pattern of consumer and producer prices established within Australia by the Wheat Board seems motivated particularly by the need for a centralised authority to operate a system which is both administratively tractable and based on well understood rules of thumb which can easily be used to deflect charges of special treatment. The concessions to both Tasmanian and Western Australian consumers can be given an obvious political interpretation, while the payment of a premium on Western Australian production represents a significant departure from the principle of pooling which probably has significant efficiency implications given the large volume of exports from that State.

# 7

# Home-Price Schemes

Where the demand for a commodity is inelastic, the withdrawal of supplies from the market will raise aggregate returns to producers. Though such a policy has no attractions for an individual agricultural producer it becomes more alluring as the group of participating producers grows larger. Attempts by voluntary farmer cooperatives, first established in Australia in dairying in the 1880s, to control supplies were generally unsuccessful. Even where a group of cooperating producers is large enough to face an inelastic demand in the short run, supply responses by non-participants are likely to make the long-run demand faced by the group elastic. Moreover, even where this is not the case, the incentive for individual producers to desert the cartel is higher the greater its success.

The most successful example of such agricultural cooperation in Australia has been the amalgamation of growers organisations which formed the Australian Dried Fruits Association (ADFA) in 1904. Operating behind a high tariff and facing a highly inelastic domestic demand, this organisation, controlling over 90 per cent of production, was able to divert supplies from the local dried vine fruit market to distilleries and from 1907 to export markets. The growth of exports to 50 per cent of production meant that a slump of 50 per cent in world prices in 1923 placed severe pressures on the voluntary home-price scheme. The initial Commonwealth reaction was to raise the tariff to protect the home price against imports and to pay an export subsidy to protect the home price against threatening grower defection from the scheme. A long-term solution was sought in regulation, with the establishment of State Dried Fruits Boards in South Australia and Victoria in 1924, a Commonwealth Export Control Board in the same year, and further State Boards in N.S.W. and Western Australia in 1927.

## State marketing boards

While diversion of supplies from the entire Australian market was the ambitious objective pursued by the ADFA, the more modest aim of diverting supplies from their State or locality held promise for the producers situated in an exporting State or region. Even where supply diversion to world markets was not profitable, the likelihood that the elasticity of interstate demand was greater than the elasticity of demand locally was very high. In these circumstances an expansion of exports interstate offered the prospect of a profitable increase in the local price up to the State's import parity.

Clearly Queensland, by virtue of climate an exporter to the rest of Australia of many agricultural commodities (tropical fruits, nuts, arrowroot, etc.), was well placed to protect its producers at the expense of its consumers by this means. Moreover where, as with sugar, it was the only significant Australian producer of a commodity with a ready international export market, the opportunity offered of unilaterally providing growers with protection at the expense of consumers nationwide.

While the Commonwealth and the States generally withdrew from the field of agricultural marketing immediately after the First World War, Queensland retained its compulsory wartime wheat pool. The Labour Party in Queensland, as elsewhere, was gratified to find agricultural producers in favour of this brand of socialism and competed actively for radical farmers' votes, while the Country Party in that State was little afflicted by the inhibitions concerning State control that governed the conservative wing of the Party in other parts of Australia at the time.

Accordingly, in 1922 a Labour government introduced the Queensland *Primary Producers Pools Act* which provided for the creation of Marketing Boards for primary commodities and the vesting of all production of a commodity in such Boards. By 1930 fourteen such commodity boards had been established, while State fruit marketing was placed under the control of a separate Committee of Direction.

These boards enforced supply diversion either through acquisition (in which case processing and marketing functions were assumed by them), through compulsory equalisation of growers' returns from different markets, or by issuing directions, either informally or via quotas, as to the markets on which disposal of the crop was permitted to occur.

Though nominally constrained by s.92 in their ability to raise local prices above import parity for the State, such Boards can in fact use their political influence or market power to this end, either by coercing major users of the commodity within the State to sign supply agreements with them at prices above import parity (e.g. Queensland wheat in the 1920s) or by dumping supplies in the local markets of interstate producers exporting to their State or otherwise threatening their interests (e.g. both the N.S.W. Egg Board in 1966, and the Victorian Egg Board in 1978, have used this sanction against producers in the Australian Capital Territory.)

Queensland enthusiasm for the principle of raising local prices to import parity - and where possible above - ran so high that two **regional** boards, for Atherton pigs and maize, were created in 1923 with the object of raising prices on the Atherton Tableland above Brisbane quotations.  Since intrastate trade could be regulated

> a Gilbertian situation developed in regard to Atherton maize.  Quantities of the grain were 'smuggled' across the boundaries of the district in defiance of the Maize Board and special regulations were, therefore, gazetted empowering members of the Board or any persons appointed by it or the police to examine within a radius of 50 miles of the boundary any vehicle believed to be carrying any of the commodity. ([35] p. 107.)

In 1927, following a conference of producer, trade union, and consumer interests, the Lang Labour government in N.S.W. passed similar legislation in the form of a Marketing of Primary Products Act.  Unlike the Queensland legislation, the N.S.W. Act provides that the machinery for the creation or dissolution of a Board on the vote of growers can be automatically activated at **their** initiative, by means of a petition to the Governor - a provision which is curious in that discretion over such decisions is the politician's major asset and the imperfections of the political capital-market might normally be expected to restrain any impulse to barter it away.

Similar Acts have been introduced in Victoria (1935) and in Tasmania (1945) while in South and Western Australia separate legislation on a commodity-by-commodity basis is required.

With the net value of a marketing board to producers largely to be found in the difference between the gains from price discrimination that it can capture and the regulatory costs that it imposes, it is understandable that proposals to establish boards for commodities **imported** into N.S.W. have often failed to command the requisite majority, while several boards for such commodities (bananas, ginger, potatoes, etc.) once introduced have been quickly voted out. [37]

## Regulation versus tax/subsidy arrangements

Since s.90 of the Constitution gives the Commonwealth exclusive power 'to impose duties of customs and excise and to grant bounties on the production of export of goods' the establishment of a home price above export parity by an individual State can be easily achieved only by regulatory means.

For the Commonwealth the situation is reversed. Regulatory imposition of Australia-wide home-price schemes by the Commonwealth has been complicated both by the need to secure the passage of complementary legislation by the States and, since 1936, by the absence of fully effective control over interstate trade. By contrast the enforcement of a home price through the tax mechanism has always been within the Commonwealth's powers and, within the constraint imposed by s.99 which requires that 'the Commonwealth shall not by any law or regulation of trade commerce or revenue give preference to any one State or any part thereof', not subject to Constitutional challenge.

Interestingly, the first Australian home-price scheme initiated by the Commonwealth, the 1926 Paterson Scheme for butter (Paterson, a Gippsland dairy farmer, was Minister of Markets in the Bruce-Page Government) though conducted without direct Commonwealth legislative support, had as its basis just such a tax/subsidy combination.

During the early years of the butter export trade the linking of local to London prices during the flush production season was viewed as a great boon by the local industry. Not only did the London market provide a floor to local prices in the summer but, by reducing the amount of storage otherwise profitable, indirectly raised local prices during the winter as well.

By the time of the establishment of the Paterson scheme however, the **full** London price (gross of export charges) had

---

[37]  See [26] Ch. 4 for a discussion of history of State Boards in Queensland and N.S.W., and [24] for an account of recent developments in N.S.W.

established itself in dairy folklore as the 'just' price below which local realisations should not fall. In the words of the originator of the scheme

> returns to the dairymen in the industry for butter sold for Australian consumption, for the greater part of the year have been governed by the value of their product on the wharf for export, i.e. London prices less all expenses incidental to export, which in effect means that the producer has to lose ocean freight, marine insurance, exchange, etc. not merely on the proportion actually exported but on every pound consumed by our own people.[38]

It was the limited objective of the Paterson scheme to relieve dairy farmers of the injustice of being required to pay such shipping charges (2.35d per lb) on produce which had never seen the inside of a ship's hold.

Participants in the scheme - that is to say, most dairy factories outside Western Australia - were to pay a levy of 1d per lb on all butter produced while a subsidy of 3d per lb was to be paid on all exports. Since about a third of production was exported at the time (1926), the funds raised by the levy were calculated to match the subsidy disbursements. Since local consumer prices would rise by 3d per lb to match the export subsidy, producer prices would rise by 2d per lb.

Being voluntary, the scheme could expect to command less united producer support the greater the gap between producer and consumer prices since that gap, equal to the production levy, represented the pay-off to a defecting producer selling his output on the domestic market.

Pressure on the gap came from the steadily rising proportion of production exported as production expanded and consumption contracted under the stimulus of the scheme. The supply response was augmented by the partial coverage of the scheme, cheese (which had originally been scheduled for inclusion) remaining unprotected, while on the demand side, local sales of butter by participating factories were eroded as supplies outside the scheme, consisting both of farm-produced butter and the production of new factory entrants, responded to the incentive of the higher home price. While the threat to the scheme posed by the commencement of imports from New Zealand could be

---

[38] Statement by T. Paterson, Minister of Markets, December 1927 (quoted in [11] pp. 469-70.)

removed by an increase in the tariff from 2d to 6d per lb in 1927, the loss of the Canadian market, where increased Australian exports were met by an anti-dumping duty, had to be endured. By 1934 exports had expanded to 54 per cent of production so that a levy of $1^3/_4$d per lb was now required to finance the 3d per lb export bounty.

As noted above, the combination of levy and bounty employed by the Paterson scheme represents one of a number of non-regulatory methods of enforcing home-price discrimination that have always been fully within the legislative competence of the Commonwealth. Three such alternatives, based on the original Paterson proportion of exports to production and equivalent in their economic impact,[39] are set out below:

|  |  | Consumption Tax | Export Subsidy | Production Tax |
|---|---|---|---|---|
| I | Production Tax + Export Subsidy | 0 | 3d | 1d |
| II | Consumption Tax + Export Subsidy | 1d | 2d | 0 |
| III | Consumption Tax + Production Subsidy | 3d | 0 | -2d |

While the first of these tax/subsidy combinations was that explicitly employed by the Paterson scheme the second formed the basis of the transfers among producers involved in the dairy equalisation arrangements that were to follow.

By 1933 the incentive to disorderly marketing under the Paterson scheme had grown so large (the levy was now equal to 20 per cent of the producer price and times were hard) that its complete disintegration threatened. The Commonwealth, having no apparent desire to see the Paterson transfers recorded in the budget statements, secured the passage of complementary Commonwealth/State legislation modelled on the dried fruits arrangements. The State legislation defined factory butter to include farm-produced butter, required all producers to be licensed, and made

---

[39] A formal demonstration of the equivalence of these fiscal alternatives is contained in Appendix 3.

provision for each dairy factory to export 55 per cent of its production from the State. The Commonwealth legislation provided for the licensing of interstate trade to ensure that this percentage was in fact exported from Australia.

It was never intended that dairy regulation should proceed according to these principles, the costs of holding each producer to a uniform export quota being considered too great. Rather, the true purpose of the legislation was to force all producers to enter into an agreement with CDPEC formed to take over from the Australian Stabilisation Committee that had administered the Paterson scheme.[40]

A recurring problem under the Paterson arrangements had been the threat to the solvency of the Stabilisation Committee arising whenever disbursements at the fixed rate of bounty appeared likely to exceed collections at the fixed rate of levy. This possibility was now to be avoided by pooling producers' returns, with sellers on local markets liable, and sellers to export markets eligible, for transfers equal to the difference between their actual realisations and the equalisation values struck at the end of each period.[41]

Under the security of the new legislation the industry was determined to exploit the tariff to the full. In 1934-35, the first year of equalisation, the local butter price was established at 7d per lb above, or about double, export parity.[42] The implicit consumption tax collected in that year by CDPEC was Ł5m (Ł4.6m on butter and Ł0.4m on cheese) and equal to 8.5 per cent of explicit Commonwealth tax revenues from all sources.

The third of the alternative tax/subsidy combinations illustrated in the table above makes the consumption tax fully explicit and would appear to suffer the greatest political disadvantage on this account. It formed the uneasy basis of Commonwealth assistance to the wheat industry between 1933 and 1940 in the shape of a tax on the domestic consumption of flour (at its height equivalent to about 60 per cent *ad valorem*) coupled with the payment of assistance to producers essentially, though not exclusively, as a bounty on

---

[40]   See Lloyd [22] pp. 49-52.

[41]   Equalisation values were originally struck monthly, were on a seasonal basis after 1942, and since 1945 have been determined on an annual basis.

[42]   Since freight from New Zealand was about 1d per lb, import parity was about 1d per lb above export parity. This, together with the tariff of 6d per lb, allowed a home price double export parity to be achieved.

wheat production.[43]

The political preference for regulation over this form of taxation was voiced by the Labour Leader, Scullin:

> I cannot see my way clear to agree to the placing of a tax on the poor in order to pay a bounty to the wealthy. A principle of justice was violated by the Government when it proposed to raise Ł1.5m by a tax on bread. There is a vast difference between an organised pool in the operation of which it is possible to clip the wings of manipulators and market riggers and to ensure that the industry is not exploited by them and one in which Parliament says that food speculators may have a free hand.[44]

---

[43] The Scullin government, concerned at the deteriorating balance of payments, embarked in 1930 on a campaign to induce farmers to 'grow more wheat', by guaranteeing 4s per bushel at sidings. The Bill incorporating the guarantee combined it with provisions for a compulsory pool and was rejected in June 1930 by the Senate, which opposed the pool. By December 1930, a Bill providing for the guarantee alone had passed the Senate but, with the Commonwealth Bank unwilling to advance the necessary funds, only Theodore's Fiduciary Note Issue Bill remained as a source of finance. That Bill was rejected by the Senate in April 1931.

Since the world gold price of wheat fell to its lowest level for 400 years in 1930-31 and since the promised guarantee had called forth a larger crop than any other achieved prior to 1960-61 the position of growers, who received from the market a price less than half the guarantee, was desperate. The Parliament which had acquired an enormous obligation to the industry commenced to pay assistance from Consolidated Revenue in 1931-32. In 1933 the flour tax was introduced to help cover the bounty and relief payments. No assistance was paid in 1936-37 or 1937-38 when wheat prices rose. While the flour tax formally continued until 1946-47, large net bounty payments to growers effectively ended in 1939-40. See [13] pp. 267-74 and pp. 480-82.

[44] Speech in House of Representatives, 1933 (quoted in [11] p. 293).

This preference was shared by the Lyons government, exposed to the odium of collecting the tax. Thus by 1935 the Commonwealth had prepared legislation which would allow home-price assistance to be delivered to the wheat industry by State Marketing Boards, again under the mantle of a system of Commonwealth licensing of interstate trade. That this legislation was not enacted was a consequence of the Privy Council decision in *James v. The Commonwealth* 1936 which destroyed the legal basis of the Commonwealth regulation of interstate trade which underpinned both the dried fruits and the dairy schemes.

The ensuing debate brought the conflict between taxation and regulation as means of home-price assistance into sharp focus. In announcing the Government's intention to seek a Constitutional amendment, s.92A, which would exempt 'laws with respect to marketing' made by the Commonwealth Parliament from the operation of s.92, Attorney General Menzies argued

> It is the policy of every party in this House to give a home consumption price to Australian farmers . . . we may attempt to give to the farmers the financial result of a home consumption price by imposing an excise duty on the commodity in question and distributing the proceeds by way of bounty . . . But if the primary industries are to be made dependent upon the occasional enactment by Parliament of excise duties and the occasional payment by Parliament of bounties it is difficult to say how there can be any stability in primary industry.[45]

On the other hand State Governments, not responsible for the tax, saw things differently:

> The flour tax is constitutional and we know where we are with it . . . The objection to it is more or less on the grounds of political expediency. If the term 'tax' is obnoxious let it be called by another name; it will smell as sweet. It could be called a home consumption price and the Commonwealth could be asked to collect it.[46]

---

[45]   Statement in House of Representatives 14 October 1936 (quoted in [11] pp. 158-59).

[46]   Speech by R.L. Butler, Premier of South Australia, Wheat Industry Conference, Canberra October 1935, (quoted in [11] p. 66).

In a similar vein, F.W. Bulcock the Queensland Minister for Agriculture, surveying the options after the referendum had been lost, observed;

> The experience in Australia in the past has not been very favourable to co-operation without legal sanction . . . Another solution would be excise and bounty. At the Adelaide meeting of the Australian Agricultural Council last August every Government in Australia agreed to the principle of excise and bounty. So the Commonwealth would not encounter any opposition from the States in bringing down a system providing for the payment of bounty and the collection of excise. The adoption of this would involve an additional charge on the Commonwealth Budget, and is not likely to be received favourably.
>    The final line of action, to speak paradoxically, would be to do nothing . . . Should this policy of *laissez-faire* be adopted Australia will become a happy hunting ground for the food speculator, and finally the people would pay the piper.[47]

The political determination to confound the twin issues of organised marketing and home-price assistance was absolute. Even though the resulting 1937 referendum was convincingly lost (64 per cent voting against and no State in favour) the search for viable forms of regulation was not abandoned.

### Home-price regulation after 1937

In the dried fruits industry, State licensing of packing sheds allowed the ADFA to buy up all but one of the licences and this has proved sufficient to sustain the home-price scheme on a 'voluntary' basis.

For wheat the solution was found in the creation in 1939 of an Australian Wheat Board exercising its powers under complementary Commonwealth/State legislation. Its relative immunity from interstate - trading problems is to be accounted for chiefly by the modest size of the margin of home over producer prices that has been established over most of the post-war period.[48] During the years 1948-49 to

---

[47]   Courier Mail 9th March 1937 (quoted in [11] pp. 493-94).
[48]   The data below are taken from Table V.2. of the BAE Submission to the IAC Inquiry into Wheat Stabilisation 1978. Figures quoted for the years 1976-77 to 1978-79 are BAE estimates.

1952-53 and 1973-74 to 1975-76 when large differentials between these prices have ruled they have been against growers, creating no problems for the Board since its control over exports is Constitutionally secure.  Similarly, over the fifteen years 1953-54 to 1967-68, the average margin of consumer prices over producer prices gross of transport and handling charges was under 4 per cent, the largest differential being 8 per cent.

Only over the years 1968-69 to 1972-73 and 1976-77 to 1978-79 have home prices been set significantly above gross returns to growers.  In the first of these period the incentive to private interstate trading provided by the 22 per cent margin of the home price over the gross price to producers established in 1967-68, was quickly countered by the introduction of separate home prices for feed and for milling wheats.  The AWB was thereby able to eliminate the differential between the home price for feed wheat and the gross return to producers while simultaneously maintaining, during 1969-70 to 1972-73, a home-price differential of approximately 15 per cent for milling wheat, in respect of which a restrictive agreement concluded with millers has mitigated the Board's private trading problems.[49]

However in recent years (1976-78 to 1978-79) the Board has again attempted to successfully combine a single home price for all wheat with a large margin (averaging about 30 per cent in 1977-78 and 1978-79) of home over gross producer prices.  The predictable result has been an upsurge in private interstate trading culminating in the High Court case *Clark-King v. Australian Wheat Board* (1978).[50]

In the case of dairying the selective payment of a

---

[49]  Millers have presumably been induced to enter into this agreement by the fact that home-prices have sometimes been held well below export, and thus grower, returns as well as by the provision of the agreement which allows millers to charge the holding costs of their stocks against the AWB.

[50]  In Clark-King the majority of the High Court felt able to conclude that the prohibition of private interstate trade in wheat was the 'only practical and reasonable manner of regulation' of such trade;  the expert opinion of the IAC *Draft Report on Wheat Stabilisation*, that all domestic trade in wheat should be set free, notwithstanding.  It remains to be seen what effect this judgement will have both on wheat pricing and on attempts to similarly regulate interstrate trade in other areas.

Commonwealth bounty has served to sustain 'voluntary' equalisation throughout the post-war period (see above pp. 19-24). Only since 1966 has the significant excess of consumer prices over returns to producers (including bounty) characteristic of a home price scheme, re-emerged. Here again State licensing of dairy factories has served to limit new entry outside the scheme and has presumably acted also as an implicit constraint upon defections by existing licence holders.

At the same time a return to the Paterson principles of tax and bounty has not been entirely avoided. In the egg industry the ability of individual State Marketing Boards to set high domestic prices was originally somewhat constrained by interstate trading. A solution here was found in 1965 with the creation of the Council of Egg Marketing Authorities of Australia through which a Commonwealth input tax (a hen levy) is paid as an export subsidy (currently $11m) to State Egg Boards.

Similarly the dairy industry has made a partial return to a Paterson basis with a Commonwealth levy on production (estimated at $62m for 1978-79) being returned as an export subsidy to the equalisation pools.

## Incidence of the implicit consumption tax

Home-price schemes have been subject to attack on several grounds. The earliest criticism, highly relevant to the political desire to obscure their effect under the cloak of organised marketing, arose out of the fact that the commodities involved (dried fruits, sugar, butter and later wheat and eggs) combine low income elasticities with their low price elasticities of demand. In consequence the apparent incidence of the large implied consumption taxes (estimated by the 1927 Brigden Report [2] to total 12.5 per cent of explicit Commonwealth taxation for sugar, dried fruits and dairy products) was highly regressive.

At the same time economists, particularly Giblin,[51] were careful to point out that the incidence of such home-price measures was more complex once allowance was made for adjustments, both to money wages, (so indexed to the cost of living as to rise more than proportionately to the general price level when the prices of basic foodstuffs rose) and to tariff protection. These repercussions, it was argued, placed

---

[51]  See for example Giblin's submission to the Gepps Royal Commission ([33], First Report, Appendix A).

the incidence of the tax substantially on producers in unsheltered traded-goods industries, chiefly in the primary sector, on fixed-income earners, and on the unemployed.

Thus, even if the supply of the home-price-protected output were completely inelastic so that there were no direct implications for resource allocation, it was reasoned that the implicit consumption tax would produce consequences similar to those of an exogenous increase in money wages - namely, a reduction in national income equal to the excess value, at world prices, over cost, of the production lost in unsheltered export industries.

Post-war academic criticism has been rather less sophisticated. The implicit consumption tax has been accepted with resignation and, with wage indexation ending in 1953, the question of its true incidence (along the lines suggested by Giblin) has not been pursued further. Rather, it has been the excess cost of the increased production induced by the implicit production bounty that has, with suitable qualification regarding the destination of the resources that would be released by its removal, attracted the attention of the critics.

This excess cost it was argued, most notably by a group of seven agricultural economists in a submission to the 1960 Dairy Committee of Enquiry [9], could be removed to the benefit of the industry and at no further cost to consumers by a two-pool scheme that distributed the proceeds of the consumption tax to producers in a lump-sum fashion on a domestic market quota, leaving any production in excess of this to the guidance of the price ruling on world markets.

In 1976 the two-pool proposal achieved official recognition. It formed the basis of two sets of IAC recommendations; one for dairy marketing [19] and the other for the industry that originated the home-price scheme - dried vine fruits [21].

# 8
## Quotas

The market entitlement or two-pool arrangement was pioneered in Australia by the sugar industry.

Administrative regulation of the sugar industry began in 1915 when, at the onset of World War I, the Queensland government acquired all sugar, selling it to the Commonwealth at a price well below import parity. The State also instituted a complex system of regulation involving price controls at all stages of production and including the statutory requirement that growers send their cane to specified mills. These arrangements survive to the present day as does the import embargo which, together with an export embargo, was simultaneously applied by the Commonwealth. All wartime sugar importation was undertaken by the Commonwealth.

The dramatic decline in acreage and production (some mills refusing to crush at the prices offered) necessitated vastly increased imports at very high world prices in 1919. In consequence 1920 saw an embarrassed Commonwealth government raise the domestic price of raw sugar by 50 per cent and abandon the field of sugar regulation.

In the years 1920-25, under the stimulus of this high price, the number of growers and acreage both increased by about 70 per cent while yields per acre almost doubled. The industry achieved export status so rapidly that by 1923 the pooling of export and domestic returns was instituted under a Queensland Sugar Board.

This Board appointed the Colonial Sugar Refinery (now CSR) together with the minor Millaquin Sugar Company Limited as its only refiners and CSR as its sole export agent, leaving CSR in the 'unfortunate' position that

> Under the arrangements between the Queensland Government and CSR the whole of the services [of transporting and refining raw sugar] . . . are carried out or arranged for by the Company at actual cost . . . [there is] . . . no element of profit for the Company . .

61

and each year a complete audit is carried out by the Queensland Auditor General to ensure that only actual costs are recovered. [52]

Freight equalisation was introduced by the establishment of a uniform wholesale price for refined sugar in all metropolitan areas, and provision was made for a rebate on the sugar in approved manufactured exports to bring this price down to import parity and for a lesser rebate to processors of fruit for domestic markets, conditional on their paying at least minimum prices for their fruit supplies. These 1923 arrangements have also endured to the present.

In 1930 the pressure placed on growers' returns by the rising proportion of production exported and by falling export prices was checked by the imposition of output quotas at the mill level (mill peaks), equal to their maximum output since 1915, and the introduction of acreage restrictions on cane farmers. Sugar produced in excess of mill peaks was, and still is, paid world prices.

It is this feature of sugar regulation that forms the basis of the proposal advanced by many agricultural economists for rationalising the system of home-price protection in other industries. [53] Of course the suggestion, that output or the employment of certain specific factors be restricted as a means of providing protection, is not in itself novel. In the case of non-traded industries and occupations where the combination of excise and production bounty (or its regulatory equivalent) would be self-defeating, and where export is not possible so that a home price scheme cannot be arranged, this is **the** method of effecting transfers from consumers to favoured producers.

## Quota negotiability

The distinguishing features of the proposed market-entitlement schemes are, first, that only the right to produce for a high-priced market, not the right to produce *per se*, is

---

[52] [38] p. 70.

[53] See the proposals for the dairy industry contained in the 'Submission by a Group of Agricultural Economists' to the Committee of Enquiry into the Dairy Industry [9] p. 125 and Drane and Edwards [12] pp. 307-17. The case for quota transferability was subsequently advanced by Gruen [16]. Parish [27] contains an analysis of the various proposals.

to be restricted, second, that the proposal is designed to replace **existing** home price protection so that it is advanced on efficiency grounds[54], and, third, that the regulatory cost that output or input controls would seem at first glance to imply is to be avoided by use of the market: specifically the economists have proposed nationwide negotiability of the rights to produce for the home market. Such negotiability, it is reasoned, will keep the regulators at bay and ensure that all output is produced at minimum cost.

Yet the history of quota schemes, and entry restrictions generally, does not appear particularly favourable to the adoption of this advocated negotiability. Moreover, it is possible to argue that the social costs of non-negotiability will be high.

Since agricultural production wanders about a good deal when free to do so, the extent of industry ossification under real-world quota arrangements can be dramatic. Between 1951-52 and 1964-65 the proportion of Australian tobacco grown in Queensland declined from 62 per cent to 49 per cent

---

[54] Mauldon and Schapper [25], arguably the most enthusiastic advocates of quota-based home-price schemes for Australian agriculture, constitute an exception. In their 'preferred agriculture',

> Generally, prices received by farmers would be without subsidies. They would be revenue maximising prices . . . They would be set in accordance with collective farmer control of supplies for both home-consumption and export markets . . . Quotas would be an integral part of our preferred policy of pricing. The home-consumption quantity would be the market supply judged to ensure the revenue-maximising price to farmers after taking into account expected export prices on the expected export quantity. Equalling the home-consumption market supply there would be negotiable home consumption quota certificates . . . The feasibility of introducing quotas into the pricing of some or all of such heterogeneous products as wool and meats is an open question . . . However feasibility studies should be made by the relevant boards of new ways of determining home-consumption and export prices for wools and meats. ([25] pp. 178-81)

(acreage: 61 per cent to 54 per cent). Over the same period Victorian production expanded from 18 per cent to 48 per cent (acreage: 19 per cent to 37 per cent) and New South Wales production expanded from 7 per cent to 9 per cent (acreage: 5 per cent to 9 per cent).[55] With the introduction of the output-quota scheme managed by the Australian Tobacco Board, State quotas were fixed in the proportions Queensland 54 per cent, Victoria 37 per cent and New South Wales 9 per cent where they have remained ever since. Not only has the southward migration of the industry been totally halted but the output-quota allocation, being on the basis of existing **acreage** proportions, effectively turned the clock back. Victorian yields were on average 11 per cent greater than those in Queensland over the years 1960-61 to 1964-65. Within States annual quotas are allocated by State Tobacco Marketing Boards in proportion to growers' existing entitlements. Farmers may trade neither quota, nor, of course, leaf.

In the case of sugar, acreage assignments, far from being negotiable, are administered in such detail that they specify the particular plots on individual farms on which sugar may be grown, neither mill nor farm peaks are transferable and since 1933 even the sale of existing farms is subject to review by the Central Cane Prices Board - 'since the granting of an assignment might lead to the inflated development of values not inherent in the land.' ([38] p. 37.) Only one new mill has been constructed since regulation began in 1915 (at which date each grower was allocated to a specific mill) and that following a Royal Commission inquiry. The number of growers which increased by 70 per cent between 1920 and 1925 has remained roughly constant since then and, needless to say, the two 1915 refiners and the monopoly marketer have not faced the rigours of entry, potential or otherwise.

Similarly, metropolitan milk quotas are non-negotiable - though they are expropriable. During 1976-77 the Dairy Industry Authority of N.S.W. cut the quotas of producers in the Base Market Quantity Area (the old Milk Zone) by about 14 per cent, transferring this quota - in line we may presume with the altering distribution of political power - to producers outside the zone.

Even where quotas are negotiable, as is the case with hen quotas **within** though not across States, the restrictions on negotiability are considerable. Consider New South Wales; here transfers must be approved by the Licensing Committee

---

[55] The data cited are taken from [7].

of the Egg Board, while the original limit of 250,000 birds per producer was recently reduced to 100,000 and is rigidly enforced (except for companies which held more than 100,000 birds at the time), companies with common directorships or managements being counted as one.

Neither restricted rice acreages nor entitlements to irrigation water generally (which are valuable because the water is sold at low prices for application to highly protected items of production) are negotiable.

Since the law of restricted quota transferability may be as well established as the law of demand, it is arguable that social-cost-cutting schemes which rest on fully and freely negotiable quotas deserve careful scrutiny.

**Advantages of non-transferability**

Quota schemes afford the opportunity for detailed administrative regulation under heavy sanction. In effect such quotas belong in part to politicians - and since they are a State responsibility this means to State politicians and the regulators they appoint.[56] The control they allow is a valuable asset which these interests cannot be expected to lightly toss away. Since the political process is not dominated by a single undifferentiated producer interest, the ability to shift the distribution of industry rents among competing claimants as the balance of marginal political influence changes is central to successful government.

The regulatory powers conferred by a quota system or by entry restrictions generally are ideally suited to this task. Consider the expropriation and transfer of N.S.W. milk quotas referred to above; this would surely have yielded lower net political benefits had quotas been transferable, not only because it would have **appeared** more expropriatory to outsiders, but also because with quotas negotiable the loss to the losers would have balanced the gain of the gainers, whereas in the circumstances of the case the latter were presumably well in excess of the former.

Concern with political balance may also be illustrated by the tendency for small quota holders to be favoured when aggregate quotas are adjusted. This was the case with the introduction of the (non-transferable) N.S.W. wheat quotas in the late 1960s,[57] with the two 10 per cent hen quota cuts in

---

[56] It is notorious that certain State politicians own a quantity of N.S.W. fluid-milk quota in fact as well as in effect.

[57] See [10] Chap. VII.

1977 and 1978, and with the milk quota expropriation referred to above.

Moreover, restrictions on negotiability can be desired by an industry at large simply because it is not in the interests of the industry as a whole to see its effective 'political size' diminish. The shifts in quota holdings between States, and their amalgamation in progressively fewer hands, that may accompany freely negotiable Australian quotas can endanger the political viability of the transfer from consumers that gives them their value, creating free-rider problems for producers in the industry concerned. The function of restrictions on negotiability is to internalise this political externality.

At the time of the introduction of hen quotas in 1974 the shift towards larger-scale production units had been proceeding for many years and could be expected to continue. Given this on-going process of change the extra capital value of negotiable over non-negotiable quotas to farmers close to the point of exit, is far greater than a static analysis predicts. In achieving quotas with limited negotiability (they sold initially for $3 per bird and now change hands at $12.50 per bird in N.S.W.) the interests of this group of small farmers prevailed.

However, as argued earlier, a transfer inefficiently delivered can be given a public-interest justification that a lump-sum transfer cannot. When a transfer is made on a permanent lump-sum basis, as with a quota, the pressure to obscure its value so that its size may be protected becomes correspondingly more acute. Non-negotiability is a prime means to this end. By way of example, in British Columbia where a negotiable fluid milk quota scheme (otherwise similar to that in N.S.W. - rustic regulation has been a major Australian invisible export) has recently come under public attack by economists, the response of the B.C. Milk Board has been to end transferability.

It would not be surprising, once the egg industry has stabilised at units of 100,000 birds each, to see negotiability ended here also.

## Domestic market quota proposals for the dairying industry

The market entitlement scheme proposed by economists to the 1960 Committee of Enquiry into the Dairy Industry [28] was a plan that, in the form recommended, guaranteed each producer a larger total profit on a smaller level of production and at no extra cost to consumers or taxpayers. With total revenue up relative to total costs no producer, it was argued, could lose. Yet the free lunch the economists had prepared was passed over by the industry.

Certain of the economists involved were evidently rather piqued by the industry's indifference, Lloyd ([23] p. 1) complaining in 1971:

> For over a decade the Australian dairy industry has had before it a proposal which offered great benefit to the economy at no cost (in fact a gain) to dairy farmers. The industry did not reject the proposals so much as ignore them . . . The advantages offered by the proposals are quite striking except apparently in the eyes of many dairy industry leaders.

Why did the industry after 1960 not quickly embrace the plan? If we are willing to impute a little foresight to certain of the 'industry leaders' an explanation suggests itself. Between 1961-64 and 1971-74 the volume of manufacturing milk produced in Australia remained unchanged.[58] The distribution of that production however altered dramatically. Production over the period fell by 48 per cent in Queensland, 41 per cent in N.S.W and 31 per cent in Western Australia. By contrast it rose by 36 per cent in Tasmania and by 24 per cent in the large producing state of Victoria. Moreover, since even in the declining States the number of dairy farms fell far faster than production - specifically by 87 per cent in N.S.W., 85 per cent in Queensland and 83 per cent in Western Australia - it is clear that certain farmers were expanding rapidly in these States also.

Clearly those producers who were rapidly expanding production could be excused for not wishing to have to purchase, from their contracting fellow farmers, the right to receive a price in excess of export parity for this additional output. If we allow that the expanding farmers may have been more influential in their industry organisations than those departing it becomes less surprising that, 'a majority of V.F.U. Executive are not, at this stage, in support of transferable quotas, i.e. freely negotiable separate from the land.' ([23] p. 2)

Indeed to argue **against** quota negotiability would seem to have been an excellent strategy for expanding farmers. There were in any case enormous political obstacles to negotiability, particularly interstate negotiability, obstacles which have still not been overcome; and the value of non-

---

[58] The data cited below are taken from [6].

negotiable quotas to farmers on the point of exit would have been relatively low.

At the same time, because average farm acreage fell over the period, there is a presumption that many small farmers stood to gain substantially from negotiable quotas, even if their transferability had been only intrastate. Why these farmers were unable to achieve the introduction of a system that would have captured them a substantial part of the present value of dairy rents, while small egg producers did achieve negotiable quotas in 1974, is a political question deserving of further study.

However any hypothetical milk-quota scheme introduced in 1960 or shortly thereafter would almost surely **not** have provided for interstate transferability. Given the massive interstate reallocation of production which eventuated it is therefore far from certain that Lloyd was correct in asserting, in 1971, that the economists had produced 'a proposal which offered great benefits to the economy'.

Furthermore, to end on a note of efficiency rather than distribution, it is unclear that the proponents of efficiency via Australia-wide quota negotiability have pushed their logic to its proper conclusion.

Consider the IAC recommendation for dairy marketing [33]. The proposal involves the movement in three stages to a situation where a production levy (currently $62m) on manufactured milk products, equal to the difference between some average of the lowest export prices and the 'chosen' home price (who, in the interests of the 'efficiency with which the community's resources are to be used'[59] shall do the choosing, the IAC does not say), is to be rebated on exports. To enable price discrimination among export markets to continue, rather less will be rebated on exports to 'preferred markets'. A market entitlement, set equal to estimated domestic consumption at the chosen home price plus planned exports to preferred markets, is to be established each period and allocated initially across farmers in proportion to the butterfat (for manufacturing) supplied by them during the three years ended June 1976. Finally that portion of the levy not rebated on exports, that is to say the sum extracted from domestic consumers and buyers in preferred export markets by the levy, will be paid by the Commonwealth direct to farmers on production within their market entitlement.

Negotiability is to be ensured by the provision that, 'a

---

[59]     Section 22 (1) *Industries Assistance Commission Act.*

farmer allocated an entitlement would be free to sell or lease part or all of his entitlement to any other **farmer** in Australia **provided the purchaser or lessee meets all the other requirements to supply milk'.** ([21] p. 27, emphasis added)

But why the restriction? Since the IAC has effectively recommended the creation of a new asset entitling the holder to a pro-rata share in that part of annual Consolidated Revenue represented by the levy funds net of disbursements on exports, **full** efficiency surely demands **full** negotiability with the requirement as to production waived so that all holders of marketable wealth have the opportunity to slot the new 'security' into their portfolios.

Would such a system of full negotiability call forth a sufficient supply of milk in all circumstances? It would certainly do so if the aggregate market entitlement were not set above the level of production which would be attained at the export price into preferred markets. Suppose however that it were set above this level. Exports into preferred markets would fall below planned levels which would be no hardship since this would indicate that prices in preferred markets were below marginal production costs on the shortfall.

Now, to take the most extreme possibility, suppose that the 'chosen' home price were low enough that domestic demand at this price exceeded the level of production at the 'average' export price. There would then be no exports and a domestic excess demand for dairy products at the fixed domestic price. But this presents no problem. The market would be happy to remove this excess demand if the domestic price were set free with the levy held fixed. Alternatively, if the levy were allowed to rise in step with the domestic price, the system would converge to a level of domestic consumption equal to production at the (notional) average export price.

Finally, if concern for consumers should demand that the originally chosen consumer price be adhered to, this is no problem either. Since it can safely be assumed that the chosen home price will be rather above import parity the Australian Dairy Corporation, with nothing, under these circumstances, but levy-collecting and product-promoting to occupy its time (there being no exports to control) could turn its hand to importing some cheap butter, cheese etc., lump its trading profits with the levy and pay the lot as a dividend to holders of the butter-bonds.

# Appendix 1

## ALLOCATION OF A SUBSIDY AMONG END-USES

The arguments in the text (pp. 18-19) can be illustrated in greater detail by considering the case of a product in perfectly inelastic supply which is used as an input in two processing industries.    The assumption of zero supply elasticity simplifies geometric exposition without detracting from the generality of the argument.

In Figure I, $O_1O_2$ represents the fixed, inelastic supply of the good:    $D_1D_1$ is the demand for it from processing industry 1, while $D_2D_1$ - to be read from right to left - is the demand from processing industry 2.    Given perfect competition, a common price of the good for both processing activities would be established at P, with industry 1 taking $O_1N$, and industry 2 taking $NO_2$, of the good.

Producers of the good could increase their revenues from sales, without changing the total quantity produced or sold, by charging different prices to the two user industries.    As is well known, revenue maximisation by this means would be achieved by charging prices such that the marginal revenues from the two markets were equalised.    In the case depicted, this involves raising the price to industry 1 and lowering it to industry 2.    Revenue maximisation thus requires that prices $P_1$ and $P_2$ be charged, and quantities $O_1M$ and $MO_2$ be sold in the respective markets.

A uniform subsidy of B dollars per unit purchased paid to all users would raise each demand curve by the same amount, leaving unchanged both the equilibrium allocation of the good between the two industries and the total net-of-subsidy revenue.    In this case of totally inelastic supply, the whole of the subsidy would be received by producers, and this would represent their total gain from the subsidy.

If, however, the subsidy were applied solely to the use of the good by industry 2, then the $D_2D_2$ curve would shift upwards (by more than B, since the subsidy expenditure would be concentrated on only part of the total production of the good) and the division of the supply between the industries would shift from N towards M. As before, the subsidy would accrue solely to producers, but their net-of-subsidy revenue would increase since they would gain more from the expanding, more elastic market 2 than they would lose from the contracting, less elastic, market 1.* This would be true of any increase in sales in market 2 up to NM, but further increases would be counter-productive, since, to the left of M, $MR_1$ exceeds $MR_2$. If, then, the funds available for expenditure on the subsidy would, if applied solely to industry 2, result in expansion of that industry's use of the good beyond $O_2M$, it would be preferable, from the producers' point of view, to apply only as much as achieved the expansion to $O_2M$, and use any residual funds to subsidise equally the good's use in each industry: this use of the residual funds would simply shift both demand curves upwards by the same amount, leaving the allocation of the product between the industries unaltered.

Thus, differential subsidisation of user industries can extract additional revenue for producers in the same way as could be achieved by the producers forming a marketing cartel and engaging in price discrimination. In addition the producers receive - in this inelastic supply case - all of the government's subsidy payments.

Figure I may also be used to elucidate the case discussed in the text of a coalition between producers and one user group. It was argued that, up to a point, it would pay the coalition to seek the exclusive subsidisation of the good in its own processing activity, regardless of the relative demand elasticities of the two user groups.

To consider the intuitively less obvious case, let us assume that the coalition involves the producers and industry 1.

The value to the **coalition** of an additional unit of the good used in industry 1 is given by the derived demand curve $D_1D_1$. (The $MR_1$ curve shows the value to **producers** of an additional unit sold to industry 1: it takes account of the transfer from producers to processors when the price has to be lowered to sell an extra unit; but such transfers net out when we consider the two groups as one coalition).

However, the value to the coalition of the sale of an additional unit to industry 2 is given by the $MR_2$ curve.

The coalition will maximise its revenue by equating its

---

* Marginal revenue in market 2 exceeds marginal revenue in market 1, as indicated by the relative heights of the $MR_2$ and $MR_1$ curves over the interval MN.

gain from **using** a unit of the good with its gain from **selling** a unit to industry 2. Diagrammatically, the optimal disposition of this good is that shown by the intersection of the $D_1 D_1$ and the $MR_2$ curves, i.e. by the allocation $O_1 R$ to industry 1 and $RO_2$ to industry 2. Such an allocation could be achieved by a subsidy paid to industry 1 sufficient to raise the $D_1 D_1$ curve so that it intercepted the $D_2 D_2$ curve at point S in the diagram.

As noted in the text, with this market allocation of the product, the price net-of-bounty in market 1, RT, equals the marginal revenue in market 2.

Although it is true that it would pay a coalition to seek, up to a point, the exclusive subsidisation of the good in its own production activity, regardless of the demand elasticities for the two user groups, it is worth noting that the relative elasticities do help determine the point up to which this strategy pays. This can be seen by reference to the diagram. A coalition between producers and industry 2 - with relatively elastic demand - could make use of a much larger exclusive subsidy than could the producer - industry 1 coalition. In the latter case the aggregate amount of subsidy payments required to implement the optimal exclusive subsidy is ST times $O_1 R$, while in the former, it is WV times $UO_2$.

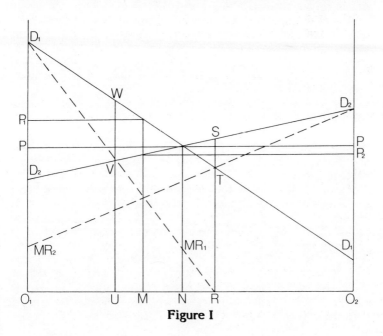

**Figure I**

# Appendix 2

## DISCRIMINATION AMONG EXPORT MARKETS

The discussion in the text (pp. 34-38) of exploitation of export markets, in the producer interest, or in the national interest, may be related to the accompanying diagrams (Figure II). Each panel depicts the same underlying supply-demand situation, but different types of intervention. In each case it is assumed that a given fixed supply, OO', of a commodity is apportioned between three markets: the home market, the demand curve of which is $D_0$, related to the origin 0; and two export markets, 1 and 2, whose demand curves net of transport costs, $D_1$ and $D_2$, are drawn in relation to the origin O'. The marginal revenue curves for each market are shown by appropriately labelled dashed lines. The curve labelled $\Sigma D$ is the horizontal summation of $D_1$ and $D_2$, while $\Sigma MR$ is the horizontal summation of $MR_1$ and $MR_2$.

Panel 1 depicts free trade. Competition ensures that supplies are distributed so as to bring about an equality of net returns (prices received by producers) in all three markets. From a national viewpoint this outcome is sub-optimal: too much of the commodity is being exported, as can be seen from the fact that the marginal revenue in each export market is less than the price, whereas the price measures the marginal valuation which home consumers place on the commodity; furthermore, the marginal revenue obtained in market 1 is much less than in market 2, so that a diversion of supply from 1 to 2 (leaving total exports unchanged) would increase export revenue.

Panel 2 illustrates the disposition of supplies among the markets with optimal intervention in the national interest, i.e. intervention designed to remedy the two defects of the free-trade situation just noted. Taxes equal to the amounts indicated by the two braces labelled $T_1$ and $T_2$ are levied on each unit of exports to markets 1 and 2 respectively These have the effects of (i) reducing export prices received by producers to the level of the marginal revenue in the export markets; (ii) equalising marginal revenue in the two export markets; (iii) reducing the home price to the new lower common net-of-tax export price, and hence making the marginal value of a unit consumed at home equal to the marginal value to the nation of a unit exported. These price changes imply a reallocation of supplies from the export markets to the home market, and a reallocation within the export market in favour of 2 at the expense of 1. (Compare Panel 2 with Panel 1 with respect to OH, $O'E_2$ and $O'E_1$ representing the quantities sold on the three markets.)

Panel 3 shows the outcome of optimal intervention from the viewpoint of producers. It is assumed here that producers are able not only to discriminate among export markets, but also between them and the home market. (The case, discussed in the text, where the latter discrimination is not possible, is considered below.) Producers maximise their returns by equating marginal revenue in all three markets. Diagrammatically, this involves finding the point of intersection of the $\Sigma MR$ and $MR_0$ curves (which shows the division of supplies between the home and export markets) and then reading off the points on $MR_1$ and $MR_2$ corresponding to the common level of $\Sigma MR$ and $MR_0$: these points show the quantities ($O'E_1$ and $O'E_2$) sold in markets 1 and 2 respectively. As compared with free trade, supplies are diverted from (and prices raised in) the relative inelastic home market and export market 1 to the relatively elastic export market 2. Total exports expand at the expense of home consumption.

Panel 4 depicts optimal intervention in the producer interest subject to the constraint that producers receive the same price in the home market as they do for exports. Whatever quantity is exported is assumed to be allocated between 1 and 2 so as to equalise marginal revenue from these markets. Corresponding to any quantity so allocated there will be an average revenue received per unit exported. This average revenue is plotted as the curve AER in Panel 4. Producers receive this common price for exports through either a pooling of export returns or a subsidy on exports to 2 financed by a tax on exports to 1. If producers are free to sell on the home or export markets, the home and export prices will tend to equality. Hence the market allocation of supplies is given by the intersection of AER and $D_0$.

In comparison with free trade we notice that - as with all the types of intervention discussed - there is a reallocation of the relative quantities of exports going to 1 and 2. In addition, there is a diversion of supplies from the home market to the export markets. This is because AER, being based on optimal exploitation of the export markets, must,

75

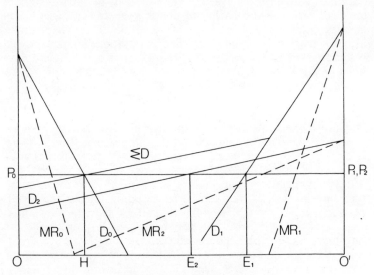

**Figure II (1) Free trade**

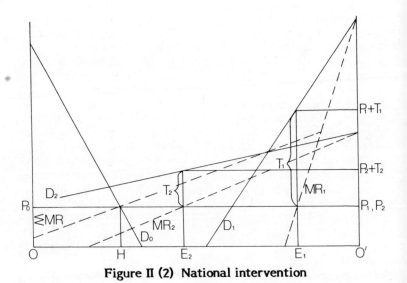

**Figure II (2) National intervention**

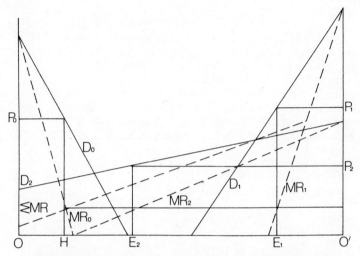

**Figure II (3) Producer intervention – unconstrained**

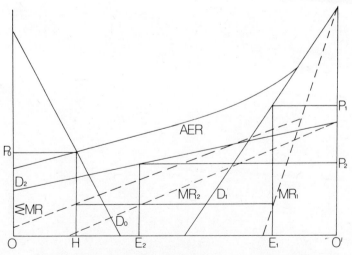

**Figure II (4) Producer intervention – constrained**

for all quantities, lie above $\Sigma D$, which shows the average revenue when exports are allocated so as to equalise the prices received in each export market. The AER-$D_0$ intersection must therefore lie to the left of the $\Sigma D$-$D_0$ intersection.

The home consumption-export market allocation in Panel 4 is intermediate between that shown in Panel 3 and free trade. This will be the case so long as in equilibrium, with the home price equal to average export returns, marginal revenue in the home market remains below export marginal revenue. If this condition were not met, the Panel 4 policy would result in **excess** diversion from the home market to export markets, as compared with the optimal diversion (from the producers' point of view) shown in Panel 3.

# Appendix 3

## PATERSON PLAN

Market equilibrium under the Paterson Plan, and the two possible variants discussed in the text, is illustrated in Figure III. DD is the home demand curve, SS the supply curve, and EE the perfectly elastic export demand curve. In the absence of intervention the domestic and export prices are identical (OE), Oq is produced, Oh consumed at home, and hq is exported. By means of various tax-subsidy schemes, the price received by producers may be raised to OF, the price paid by consumers to OC, with resulting expansion of production to OQ, exports to HQ, and contraction of home consumption to OH. As illustrated, these schemes are self-financing, the tax collected being equal to the subsidy disbursed.

The taxes and subsidies are composed of various combinations of the rectangular areas labelled, a, b, c, and d, as follows:

I.    (Paterson Plan) export subsidy, b+d; production tax, a+b

II.    export subsidy, d; consumption tax, a.

III.    production subsidy c+d; consumption tax, a+c.

The logic of these schemes is seen most clearly in II. Since the home price adjusts to the price received for exports, a subsidy paid on exports increases producers' receipts by a multiple of the subsidy payments, the gearing factor being the ratio of total production to exports. A tax is then levied on home consumption at such a rate that it raises sufficient revenue to pay the export subsidy. Hence for this scheme to be self-financing, area a must be equal to area d. Schemes I and III produce the same result but involve additional money transfers of areas b and c respectively.

The diagram also serves to illustrate the fourth variant, a home-price scheme, under which the home-consumption price

79

is set at OC, and producers receive a price, OF, equal to the average return in the home and export markets. Area a then represents equalisation payments by sellers in the home market and area d equalisation receipts by sellers in the export market.

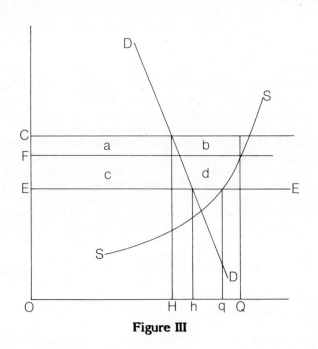

**Figure III**

---

## LIST OF ABBREVIATIONS

ADFA   Australian Dried Fruits Association
AMB    Australian Meat Board
APC    Apple and Pear Corporation
AWB    Australian Wheat Board
AWC    Australian Wool Corporation
BAE    Bureau of Agricultural Economics
CDPEC Commonwealth Dairy Produce Equalisation
       Committee
IAC    Industries Assistance Commission

# References

1. Board of Inquiry into the Dairy Industry in Victoria, *First to Fifth Reports*, Melbourne, 1975-1977

2. Brigden, J.B. *et al*, *The Australian Tariff: An Economic Enquiry*, Macmillan, 1929

3. Buchanan, J.M. and Tullock, G., 'Polluters' Profit and Political Response: Direct Controls versus Taxes', *American Economic Review*, March 1975

4. Bureau of Agricultural Economics, *Cotton Growing in Australia*, Canberra, 1963

5. Bureau of Agricultural Economics, *The Australian Cotton Growing Industry*, Canberra, 1970

6. Bureau of Agricultural Economics, *The Australian Dairyfarming Industry*, (1971-72 to 1973-74), Canberra, 1975

7. Bureau of Agricultural Economics, *The Australian Tobacco Growing Industry*, (1970-71 to 1972-73), Canberra, 1976

8. Callaghan, A.R., *The Wheat Industry and Stabilisation*, Department of Primary Industry, Canberra, 1972

9. *Committee of Enquiry into the Dairy Industry*, Commonwealth Government Printer, Canberra, 1960

10. Connors, T., *The Australian Wheat Industry: Its Economics and Politics*, Gill Publisher, Armidale, 1972

11. Copland, D.B. and Janes C.V., *Australian Marketing Problems*, Angus & Robertson, Sydney, 1938

12. Drane, N.T. and Edwards, H.R. (eds), *The Australian Dairy Industry*, Cheshire, Melbourne, 1961

13. Dunsdorfs, E., *The Australian Wheat Growing Industry 1788-1948*, MUP, Melbourne, 1956.

14. Freebairn, J.W. and Gruen, F.H., 'Marketing Australian Beef and Export Diversification Schemes', *Australian Journal of Agricultural Economics*, April 1977

15. Graham, B.D., *The Formation of the Australian Country Parties*, ANU Press, Canberra, 1966

16. Gruen, F.H., 'Crying Over Spilt Milk', *Economic Record*, September 1961

17. Harris, S., Crawford, J.G., Gruen, F.H. and Honan, N.D., *The Principles of Rural Policy in Australia: A Discussion Paper* (Rural Green Paper), AGPS, Canberra, 1974

18. Industries Assistance Commission, *Dairy Industry*, AGPS, Canberra, October 1975

19. Industries Assistance Commission, *Dairy Industry Marketing Arrangments*, AGPS, Canberra, September 1976

20. Industries Assistance Commission, *Fruitgrowing Part B: Apples and Pears*, AGPS, Canberra, January 1976

21. Industries Assistance Commission, *Fruitgrowing Part C: Dried Vine Fruit*, AGPS, Canberra, January 1976

22. Lloyd, A., 'The Marketing of Dairy Produce in Australia', *Review of Marketing and Agricultural Economics*, March 1950

23. Lloyd, A., Quotas: Some General Issues, with Particular Reference to the Dairy Industry. Paper delivered at Australian Agricultural Economics Society Conference, Adelaide, 1971

24. Longworth, J.W., 'The Problem of Meat Marketing: Are Marketing Boards the Answer?', *Australian Quarterly*, March 1972

25. Mauldon, R.G. and Schapper, H.P., *Australian Farmers Under Stress in Prosperity and Recession*, University of Western Australia Press, Nedlands, 1974

26. Morey, J.A., *The Role of the Statutory Marketing Board in the Organised Marketing of Australia's Primary Products*, University of Sydney, Sydney, 1959

27. Parish, R., 'The Costs of Protecting the Dairy Industry', *Economic Record*, June 1962.

28. Peltzman, S., 'Towards a More General Theory of Regulation', *Journal of Law and Economics*, August 1976

29. Pincus, J.J., *Pressure Groups and Politics in Antebellum Tariffs*, Columbia University Press, New York, 1977

30. Posner, R.A., 'Taxation by Regulation', *Bell Journal of Economics and Management Science*, Spring 1971

31. Reeves, W.P., *State Experiments in Australia and New Zealand*, Grant Ritchards, London, 1902 (Republished Macmillan, Melbourne, 1969)

32. *Report of Royal Commission of Inquiry into the Fruit Industry of New South Wales*, Legislative Assembly of N.S.W., March 1939

33. Royal Commission on the Wheat Flour and Bread Industries, *Report*, Government Printer, Canberra, 1932-34.

34. Shann, E., *An Economic History of Australia*, CUP, Cambridge, 1948

35. Smith, W.M., *The Marketing of Australian and New Zealand Primary Products*, Pitman, London, 1936

36. Stigler, G.J., 'The Theory of Regulation', *Bell Journal of Economics and Management Science*, Spring 1971 (Reprinted in [37])

37. Stigler, G.J., *The Citizen and the State; Essays on Regulation*, University of Chicago Press, Chicago, 1975

38. Sugar Inquiry Committee, *Report on the Australian Sugar Industry*, 1952

39. Trade Practices Commission, *Report on Packaging and Labelling Laws in Australia*, AGPS, Canberra, 1977

40. Twohill, R.J.J., *Epitome of Dairying Industry Organisations in Australia*, CDPEC, Sydney, 1956

# Index

85